EDUCATION
3.0

Seven Steps to Better Schools

James G. Lengel

Foreword by David Steiner

Teachers College, Columbia University
New York and London

Published by Teachers College Press, 1234 Amsterdam Avenue, New York, NY
10027

Credits and permissions for figures and tables appear on page 113.

Library of Congress Cataloging-in-Publication Data

Lengel, James G.
  Education 3.0 : seven steps to better schools / James G. Lengel; foreword by
  David Steiner.
     p. cm.
  Includes bibliographical references and index.
  ISBN 978-0-8077-5382-8 (pbk.)—ISBN 978-0-8077-5383-5 (hardcover)
     1. School improvement programs. 2. Educational technology. I. Title. II.
     Title: Education three point zero.
  LB2822.8.L47 2012
  371.2'07--dc23   2012026789

ISBN 978-0-8077-5382-8 (paperback)
ISBN 978-0-8077-5383-5 (hardcover)

Printed on acid-free paper

Manufactured in the United States of America

20   19   18   17   16   15   14   13   8   7   6   5   4   3   2   1

Contents

Foreword

We have all heard the call for a new, 21st-century education, the kind that will provide our children with the skills and knowledge they will need in a new economy founded on knowledge and services. We can largely agree on what this new education *shouldn't* look like: rows of desks anchored in place while teachers lecture to bored students, rote memorization from heavy textbooks in preparation for multiple choice tests, a "computer room" hidden away somewhere in a school, empty gestures to "critical thinking" and "metacognitive skills" that are little understood and even less implemented in our teaching or curriculum. But beyond the rhetoric of technology and change, it is much harder to define what this call truly means for those on the front line of delivering education to America's 54 million K–12 public students. What Jim Lengel does in the book before you is to strip away that rhetoric, move past the hackneyed clichés of the new teacher-speak—"the guide on the side" or the "peer in the rear"—and paint a portrait of what the new learning environment can actually look like and, just as importantly, how to get there.

Jim understands that it takes a whole district—administrators, principals, and teachers, as well as the parents, students and politicians—to institute the necessary full-scale planning and redesign work. While a single teacher can (and often does) perform minor miracles in her or his classroom, Jim knows that only such systemic reform will change the learning environment at real scale. He understands that teaching students to achieve self-directed learning; enabling them to conduct deep research around truly challenging topics; supporting them in team approaches to problem solving; encouraging them to become authors of their work in multimedia environments; creating 24/7 learning opportunities that explode the 19th-century conception of classroom periods defined by bells and managed by a single teacher, that all of this cannot be achieved by a single teacher or school in isolation. Jim begins by echoing the call to transform the topography of education, but he goes on to give it new meaning by showing just how we can reimagine, redesign, and then rebuild the learning environment for our age.

Why should we listen? Well, the short answer is that those who have—across America, in China, in France, in South America—keep asking Jim to do more, to teach more policy makers and educational administrators and teachers what a 21st-century education actually looks like. From Apple to Cisco, New York City to Mesa, Arizona, Jim has been tested in practice and rewarded by continued demands for his expertise by those who can, in many instances, pick just about anybody.

So when Jim writes about the steps required to transform our learning environments in the United States, he is not an arid academic or armchair consultant dispensing platitudes. Jim has walked the walk. He has delivered on this vital reform agenda in a plethora of places, and with extraordinary success. I have been delighted to have added myself—as dean of one of the oldest public schools of education in the country—to this list. Here at Hunter College in the City University of New York, Jim designed and again, just as importantly, worked with me to embed into our practice what has become a national model for the video analysis of future teachers.

Reading this book is thus not an experience in creative fiction nor fantasy, but a reality check on what it will take to provide our students with a very different kind of education—and a reality check can be less fun than rhetoric. The process of engineering serious transformation in our public schools is grinding hard work, full of potential pitfalls from pedagogical, economic, or political perspectives. Careless assumptions about the process can doom it from the start; neglected constituents can do the same throughout the lifetime of the reform initiatives. Jim does not sugarcoat the process: Reading this book is also a reminder about just how difficult it is to make systemic change in our schools.

But it is also a success story. The narratives of change that Jim conveys are real, and the lessons he draws are correspondingly important. While not every ingredient in every recipe may end up on your list, policy makers and stakeholders committed to transforming our schools will find this book invaluable in explaining to themselves and their peers what they are doing, and why they are doing it.

Finally, for those who enjoy the deep questions, Jim's book will raise more—thoughtfully and provocatively—than it can answer: What should an education for democracy look like? What happens to our cherished narratives about history and country when the traditional authority of the teacher is transformed? How will more self-directed students master the self-discipline on which higher-order thinking is directed? What will happen as we discover that the very idea of a bricks and mortar school may itself be made redundant in our new vision of education? There is much here that deserves our sustained attention. Certainly, no matter how carefully we make the change to new forms of learning, something will be lost—as it was when we moved from the pen to the typewriter—and some of these deep questions will remain as hard to answer as they ever were.

But Jim has undoubtedly set out a road map to that much talked-about but rarely glimpsed destination: the new educational system. Our students, living in a world saturated by multimedia messages, open-architecture online environments, and instant access to trillions of pieces of information, cannot be treated as if they are sitting in one-room schoolhouses on the prairie. We can stumble our way forward, or we can learn from the pragmatic and hard-earned wisdom of Jim Lengel, who has done more effective thinking about how to make 21st-century learning a reality for our children than anyone I know.

—*David Steiner*

Acknowledgments

Thousands of people have contributed to the writing of this book, and many have supported and encouraged my work on the ideas of Education 3.0. My colleagues at Hunter College, Cisco, and Apple have provided opportunities to work with faculties around the world who are working toward new forms of teaching and learning. My family has been patient with my travel to far-off schools and my self-absorbed writing.

But the most important acknowledgment goes to the leaders, teachers, and students of the many schools and colleges that I have visited and worked with as they invent Education 3.0, including:

Alabama State University
American International School of Guangzhou, China
Ballston Spa School District, New York
Calallen High School, Texas
Cambridge School of Weston, Massachusetts
Canadian International School, Hong Kong
Catoosa School District, Oklahoma
Chinese International School, Hong Kong
City Polytech, New York
Clark Atlanta College, Georgia
Cleveland Art Institute, Ohio
Global Learning Collaborative, New York
Global Tech Prep, New York
Grace Dodge High School, New York
Coppell High School, Texas
Harlem Success Academy, New York
Hebrew Day School, Baltimore
Herschel School, New York
Hyde Park Elementary School, Vermont
International School of Beijing, China
iSchool, New York
Jefferson Parish School District, Louisiana
Korean International School, Hong Kong

Long Beach Preschool, New York
Massachusetts Elementary School Principals Association
McGlone Elementary School, Denver
Mesa Unified School District, Arizona
Mitchell College, North Carolina
National School Boards Association
New York City Department of Education
Ocean University of Tsingtao, China
Ørestad Gymnasium, Copenhagen, Denmark
Paul D. Camp College, Virginia
Pennfield School, Rhode Island
Rantzausminder Efterskole, Denmark
Rhode Island Principals Association
Science Leadership Academy, Philadelphia
SENAI School of the Future, Florianopolis, Santa Catarina, Brazil
Shenandoah University, Virginia
South China University of Technology, Guangzhou, China
South Kent School, Connecticut
Texas Association of School Administrators
The Cinema School, New York
Thomas Jefferson High School, Virginia
University of Nantes, France
Valhalla School District, New York
Valverde Elementary School, Denver
Windham High School, New Hampshire

. . . and many others who have dared to dream and build the schools they need.

EDUCATION
3.0

Seven Steps to Better Schools

Introduction

The schools we have are not the schools we need. Not if we want to compete successfully in the global economy, not if we want all our citizens to enjoy the blessings of understanding, not if we want to take full advantage of the information technologies we have recently invented. We need schools that match the needs of tomorrow, but a quick survey shows that we have very few of them.

Our best schools, measured by standards a century old, fail to prepare students for the new world they will face when they graduate. Our worst schools meet neither the old standards nor the needs of the new world, and see few of their graduates work through to success. We need new schools that send students off with what they need to succeed in their generation, and we need new standards and measurements that are based on the needs of the world and the workplace.

Education 3.0 paints a picture of what these schools should look like and then guides you along the process of envisioning your own new school. It begins with a look back at how schools in the past have reflected the societies they serve, and how that reflection has become tarnished in the last few years. Then it looks to the possibilities offered to us today, taking full advantage of the new digital information technologies. You'll glimpse Education 3.0 on the ground, through the eyes of a student, a teacher, and a school leader. You'll examine in detail the new infrastructures, both educational and technical, that underlie this revised school. Finally, when you are ready to revise your own school, *Education 3.0* provides an array of tools to create a new vision, write a comprehensive plan, and implement the changes.

Along the way, you'll visit students, teachers, and schools that are practicing the principles of Education 3.0 today. Not just in the wealthy suburbs, but in the boondocks and innermost areas of cities. You'll hear from them firsthand of their struggles and their successes.

SCHOOLS TODAY

Imagine an automobile factory where 100 cars start out on the assembly line on Monday morning, but along the way 40 of them are lost. So on Friday only 60 cars roll off the line ready for customers. Imagine further that the customers do not seem satisfied with those 60 cars and would buy them only with big discounts from the list price—and complain about them as long as they owned them.

Not even General Motors in its recent recalcitrant recession fell this far. A factory like this would never survive in the marketplace. Its management, stockholders, and employees would see the writing on the wall and work together to improve the results. If they didn't, customers would stop buying their cars, and they'd soon go out of business.

Now imagine a high school where 100 freshmen start out in the 9th grade, but along the way 40 are lost. So on graduation day at the end of 12th grade only 60 line up to get their diplomas. Imagine further that the employers and college faculty who receive these students do not seem satisfied with their preparation, and take them only because no better graduates are available, complaining constantly about their quality.

In many of our large cities, these schools are easy to find. Table I.1 shows the percentage of ninth graders reaching graduation in a sample of large cities.

While wealthy suburban districts see a larger proportion of seniors in the graduation line, the national average graduation rate of 71% is not a sign of success.[1] And those students who stick it out are not nearly as engaged in their studies as they used to be, nor do they see school as very useful to their preparation for the future.[2]

For the first time in American history, the overall high school graduation rate is falling. A century ago, very few Americans completed high school; in 1905, about 5% of the eligible 18-year-olds got diplomas. The percentage increased with the decades: 10% in 1910, 20% in 1920, 50% in 1950, to almost 90% in 1990. Thus the 20th century saw a continuous and progressive climb in the proportion of citizens completing high school. Universal high school education, at public expense, was an important element in the American dream.[3]

In 1990 the graduation rate leveled off, and is now falling. As a century of educational progress recedes, we need to ask why. Professionals and pundits offer many seemingly contradictory reasons for the decline (see Table I.2).

Some of these factors may certainly contribute to the results we see. But in addition to being self-contradictory and focused as much on assigning blame as solving the problem, they miss two important factors:

TABLE I.1. Percentage of Ninth-Grade Students Who Graduate from High School in Large Cities

City	Percentage
Austin	59
Baltimore	42
Chicago	51
Cleveland	34
Detroit	38
Fresno	52
Los Angeles	44
Memphis	51
New York	51
San Diego	64

TABLE I.2. Contradictory Reasons for Decline in Graduation Rates

Reason A	Reason B
The low quality of teaching due to poor preparation and the stranglehold of teacher unions	The micromanagement and deprofessionalization of the craft of teaching
The social and economic problems of our cities and minority youth	Inefficient urban school district bureaucracies and weak leadership
The lack of common national curriculum and standards	The rigidity and irrelevance of the standard curriculum
Lack of frequent and accurate assessment of student achievement	Too much time spent testing, not enough time learning
The lack of clear standards for graduation from high school	The effect of high-stakes exit-testing on students' hopes for graduation
The lack of parental control over their child's education	Working parents who don't pay enough attention to their children's' education
Too many local school boards meddling in the management of schools	Not enough local control over the management of schools
The failure of schools to take advantage of new media developments	The distractions of the commercialized mass media

- Dynamic intelligence and energy of today's students
- Radically altered nature of the workplace that has been brought about over the last two decades by digital information technologies

These two related factors, ignored by many schools and most education reformers over the last 30 years, explain the declines in completion and interest better than any of the reasons listed in Table I.2, all of which have been around for decades, have had little effect when tried, and ignore the world outside of school as well as the nitty-gritty of the teaching and learning that actually goes on in the classroom.

The Great Debate

When I was very young, I visited Bobby down the street to play with his boxing toy (see Figure I.1). When we wound it up, the two fighters in the ring would move around and punch each other. They never fell down, and no boxer won the match; we just sat and watched them swing at each other until the spring gave out.

The current national debate in K–12 education is like that. The two sides, well-defined now for two decades, slug it out in a very public and predictable match. One side complains about the poor performance of urban students, blames the teachers' unions, and calls for more multiple-choice tests to prove their point. The other side defends the status quo, blames the students, and calls for fewer tests and more money. Each side calls the other bad names, just as boxers are heard to curse in the ring. Their tactics have descended to such antics as painting scatological slogans on the Idaho education commissioner's pickup truck[4] and doctoring exam papers so that their district scores increase. Neither side wins.

Meanwhile, schools remain pretty much as they were before the debate started. Neither side of the great debate proposes to build schools suited to the future; in fact, most of their model schools look and work very much like the schools I attended in the 1950s. During the debate years, the experience of a student has changed little, except for more multiple-choice tests. Graduation rates, international comparisons, and student satisfaction have actually fallen during this time.[5]

Education 3.0 is part of a grass-roots attempt to help schools rise above this scatological repartee, ignore the question of blame, and get on with the necessary work of building better schools. The schools involved in this process want to engage students, strengthen teaching, connect learning, advance assessment, and transform the process of schooling. That's what we're about in Education 3.0.

FIGURE I.1. Boxing Toy.

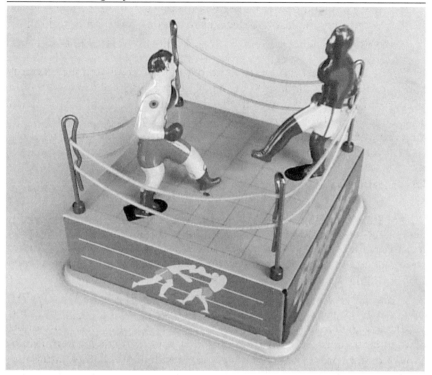

Engage Students. Students perform better when they are engaged in their studies, when they see the relevance of what they learn, and when they hold in their hands all the tools they need to learn efficiently. In many of our schools, we see little of this engagement. The National Study of Student Engagement and the United States Department of Education's annual High School Student Survey show a steady decline in students' connection with their school. But when the principles of Education 3.0 are deployed to empower students to search, collaborate, and create, they perform better and their attitudes improve. How to engage students?

- Challenge them with assignments that aim at important issues and call for combining skills and knowledge from many subjects.
- Provide them with the tools necessary to learn—modern tools, as are used in the laboratory and business.
- Enable them to connect to the resources they need, most of which are available online.

- Permit them to learn and earn credit at times and places beyond the school day.

Strengthen Teaching. If we teach as we did 10 or 30 or 50 years ago, our students will not be prepared to compete with their peers in the rest of the world. We can take advantage of online resources, web conferencing, and digital classroom tools to enable teachers to learn new ways, and to employ them in school. We need not close school in order to renew our teachers' skills; but we do need to reorganize the use of space and time to permit them the flexibility for professional growth within their workday. How to strengthen teaching?

- Use technology to relieve teachers of some of the paperwork and custodial care assignments that consume teachers' time.
- Provide them with the tools necessary to learn and practice new ways of teaching.
- Enable them to connect to the resources and people they need in order to learn new skills and build the new curriculum.

Connect Learning. To succeed in today's academic and business environments, our students need to be able to use the digital information resources that grease the worlds of higher learning and commerce. To be prepared for an increasingly global economy, they need to learn to live and work with people from distant cultures and unknown languages. To be competitive with their peers, they need to be able to use the World Wide Web as a library and learning center. How to connect learning?

- Ensure that every student has full access to the information available online and knows how to use it responsibly.
- Provide students daily practice with the standard tools of connectivity and collaboration: e-mail, search, messaging, web conferencing, and streaming video.
- Build industrial-strength, standards-based networks in our schools and let students and teachers use them for their academic work.

Advance Assessment. If we limit our measures of student performance to the multiple-choice tests of 50 years ago, we will have no idea whether they have learned what they need to succeed. What we measure, and how we measure it, must take full advantage of current networked digital information technologies. Ubiquitous technology in the hands of students will permit us to track their progress more frequently, embedding assessment into their day-to-day assignments, and, more comprehensively, to measure the full gamut of skills necessary for success. How to advance assessment?

- Put our paper-based learning resources and assignments online so they can be more easily accessed by students and updated by teachers.
- Embed frequent assessments into these assignments, both self-correcting and performance-based.
- Develop a new technology of comprehensive assessment that is not based on the restrictions of the bubble test.

Transform process. The way we do things in school is based often-times on the technologies of the past: paper, pencil, book, and lecture hall. Many of these procedures waste the time and energy of students and teachers that would be better spent in learning. Tasks such as taking attendance or handing out paper or administering bubble tests or checking out books or listening to a lecture can be eliminated or reduced through the careful application of technology. Technology has transformed the day-to-day processes of the world outside of school; let's take advantage of these tools to do things more efficiently in school. How to transform process?

- Move from paper-based to online systems for registration, attendance, grading, and communication.
- Put lecture material online in varied forms (text, audio, images, video) for students to absorb on their own, and use class time for discussion and deeper development of ideas.
- Put mobile digital devices in the hands of all teachers and students to enable them to learn anytime, anyplace, and in any medium, as well as to handle the administrative tasks associated with school.

So let's stop fighting with each other, get out of the boxing ring, and channel the energy of our leadership toward the tasks of engaging students, strengthening teaching, connecting learning, advancing assessment, and transforming school processes. And let's take advantage of technology to help us.

Education 3.0

This book shows how the American K–12 school is not well adapted to the nature of the modern workplace or to the lives and minds of today's students. It calls on educators to take advantage of modern information technologies, understand the changes in the nature of today's workplaces, apply recent knowledge of how students learn, capitalize on the energy and industry of our students, and move from education version 2 (Education 2.0) to education version 3 (Education 3.0). The book begins not in the cabinet rooms of the policy makers, nor in the cloisters of the researchers, nor in the panel discussions of the pundits, but in the once and future classrooms full of students. And it looks at school from their perspective.

In fact, the foundation of Education 3.0 is built on the student's perspective of school. The hundreds of schools and districts around the world that have gone through the process of change described in this book all began by envisioning what their transformed school would look like through the eyes of a student. Each school developed a story, *A Day in the Life of a Student*. This story served throughout the rest of the process as the basis for the transformation. You'll read several of these Day in the Life stories as you work through the book and find a few more in Appendix A.

The Day in the Life stories paint a picture of a school that does indeed prepare students for the modern world of work and university study, and at the same time capitalizes on the energy and industry of young people and takes full advantage of networked digital technologies. They were authored not by pundits, policy makers, or politicians, but by students, teachers, parents, and citizens working together to reinvent and build the schools they need.

The development of the Day in the Life story is the second of seven steps that move a school toward Education 3.0.

SEVEN STEPS TOWARD EDUCATION 3.0

Education 3.0 takes a school through a seven-step planning process that helps it transform itself into a community that is well matched to the needs of the new economy, capitalizes on energies of youth, and takes full advantage of networked digital technologies. The process helps the school envision a more powerful educational model, and provides tools to plan for its implementation and guidance in making it happen. Here are the seven steps:

1. Recognize the need for change
2. Set the vision
3. Scan the system
4. Plan for action
5. Adopt the plan
6. Build Education 3.0
7. Monitor and refresh

Education 3.0 includes both educational and technical planning: It first helps the school community develop and articulate its educational needs and dreams, and then helps it design a plan for technologies and policies that will support those. The focus throughout is on students, learning, and teaching. The aim is to transform these to fit the needs of the new economy, the capabilities and aspirations of youth, and the educational possibilities of networked digital technologies. In this chapter we give an introduction to the steps and how they might happen in a sample school district. The remainder of the book guides the school community through each step in turn.

Step 1: Recognize the Need for Change

This step helps the school answer some basic questions:

- What is Education 3.0?
- What does it look like in practice?
- What does it take to get there?

The purpose of this step is to help the school's leadership understand the nature of educational transformation and determine whether they are ready for it. It's intended to be an eye-opener, a projection of the art of the possible in education. It provides the motivation for the rest of the process, by explaining Education 3.0 in its historical context and then showing concrete examples of what the transformation can look like from the point of view of a student, a teacher, and a district leader. At this step the school community begins to understand the curricular, technical, and policy changes necessary to support Education 3.0. Case studies drawn from on-the-ground experience provoke the community to discuss the implications for their own school. Appendix C contains four case studies of schools using Education 3.0.

Step 2: Set the Vision

At this step in the process the school builds a vision of a day in the life of a student at its transformed school. Guided by the ideas of Education 3.0 learned at Step 1, the faculty and leadership paint a picture of the possibilities teaching and learning at their school. The vision is carefully crafted to illustrate the new forms of teaching and learning, the updated curriculum, the revised policies, and the central role of network technologies called for by Education 3.0. The school community examines more closely the educational activities of students and teachers in Education 3.0, gathers the key ideas and illustrative examples of transformed learning, and creates a multimedia description of a day in the life of a student at its transformed school. The vision is built by teams of educators working with students, parents, school board members, and businesspeople. The result is a multimedia presentation, as well as a text document, suitable for communication with students, parents, faculty, and the community. This book provides several sample visions from schools that have gone through the process.

Step 3: Scan the System

In this step the community examines its schools as they are today, comparing them with their vision of the future. The book provides an array of surveys and questionnaires to assist in this process. Students, faculty, and the community all take part in the scan of the schools, helping to uncover exemplary practices as well as opportunities for improvement. Resources for this step include an Education 3.0 Inventory, a Technical Infrastructure Analysis, an Educational Infrastructure Analysis, and a Faculty Technology Profile.

Step 4: Plan for Action

At this step the school community composes a detailed plan to bring its vision to reality. Based on the findings of the system scan, the school sets forth the changes in the technical and educational infrastructures that are necessary to support the Day in the Life story that they envisioned earlier in the process. The plan is drawn up by a team of teachers, students, school leaders, technical experts, and community members.

Tools for this step include an educational planning template, a technical planning template, samples from actual schools, and background briefings on relevant technologies. The plan includes a budget, a date, and a responsible person for each item of transformation.

Step 5: Adopt the Plan

At this step school leaders communicate the plan, build support in the community, and get final approval. In most jurisdictions in the United States and around the world, the kind of transformation called for in Education 3.0 will require a substantial public investment in education, in the form of a bond vote or an allocation of funds from a ministry or legislature. The community learns at this step how to generate a report to the community from the information gathered earlier and how to create a multimedia slide show to build support.

Step 6: Build Education 3.0

As the school implements its plan over a year or two, this book guides them along the way with technical consultation, educational advice, and ideas for professional development. It advises the school as it proceeds along two parallel tracks of transformation, technical and educational, with tools for identifying dependencies and tracking progress. The resources at this step include advice on many aspects of their transformation, from routing protocols to curriculum planning, from projectors to professional development, from iPads to interdisciplinary units.

Step 7: Monitor and Refresh

At this step the school tracks the progress of the transformation process and refreshes the plan as needed to reflect new conditions. The book includes tools for surveying students, teachers, and community on movement toward the vision, and advice on updating the plan as new technologies offer new potential to the school's vision and plan.

TWO YEARS IN THE LIFE

What do these seven steps look like in practice? To help you get a feel for what to expect, read this story of a sample district's progress, drawn from the experiences of a dozen actual cases. We'll call the combined sample Carson Unified School District. We join the district 2 years ago, while they were still in the era of Education 2.0, and follow them as they go through the process of awareness, planning, and transformation.

Step 1: Recognize the Need for Change

> The district realizes it's not preparing its students for the lives they'll lead in the 21st century. As the world outside of school changes, especially with the application of new technologies to the workplace, the schools may not have adapted. This recognition happens in many ways, most often with an impetus from the community outside of the normal channels.

September of Year 1. At the district's school board meeting, Superintendent Hunter reports on her participation in the annual State Leaders conference, at which she heard Tony Wagner speak on his book, *The Global Achievement Gap.*[6] The next item on the agenda is a petition from the Student Council asking the board to stop buying textbooks and shift instead to digital curriculum materials. And then during the public part of the meeting, the personnel director at the local General Electric plant reports how Carson High School students are not doing as well on the new employment screening tests.

After a discussion among the board members, noting the convergent nature of these last three items, the superintendent proposes to the board a voluntary task force to look more deeply into how well the schools are preparing students for the 21st century.

Step 2: Set the Vision

Educators and community in the district work together to paint a picture of what education should look like. With advice and provocation from partners in business, industry, and academia, they imagine what school needs to be like to produce the kinds of students who will succeed in college and work during their lifetimes. As they do their work, they go out of their way to practice and model Education 3.0 principles, communication methods, and technologies.

October of Year 1. The school board votes to empower a task force to recommend to them a revision of the focus of education in the district. It's made up of volunteers: a student, a parent, two teachers, a recent graduate, and a local businesswoman. The board charges them to seek input, draw up a vision, and report back, led by Superintendent Hunter. It votes a small budget for visits and administrative help for the task force.

Hunter finds a principal from a neighboring district who needs an internship project for his degree in educational leadership. She convinces him to serve as staff for the task force, arranging its communications, doing its research, and generally keeping it on track. A retired accountant from the community agrees to serve as its secretary and bookkeeper.

November of Year 1. The Vision Task Force meets, sets goals for itself, collects ideas from many places, and visits neighboring schools following 21st-century practices. They hear of a school in Denmark, Ørestad Gymnasium, built expressly around Education 3.0 ideas. They ask their exchange student, studying just across the Øresund in Sweden, to visit the school and send back her findings. Two weeks later the Danish principal invites them to a live video walk-through of the school through WebEx.

Carson Unified joins the Partnership for 21st-Century Skills, and takes advantage of their online network and resources. Hunter meets (by Telepresence) with the state's deputy commissioner of education to see how much leeway they have to bend state regulations and policies as they implement their vision. She learns that while there's no way to avoid the state accountability tests, the state economic development office does offer incentive grants for innovative high schools.

January of Year 1. Having worked throughout the fall and winter, the Vision Task Force completes its report, entitled *Carson 3.0,* and publishes it as a multimedia presentation, a podcast, and a brochure. The first part of it imagines and describes a *Day in the Life of a Carson Student,* and the second part explains the rationale. The school board schedules public hearings on the vision, and members of the Vision Task Force present it to their various constituencies: students, faculty, parents, business leaders, and community.

February of Year 1. Endorsements of *Carson 3.0* trickle in from various groups: the teacher's association, the Rotary Club, the PTA, the Student Council, the Chamber of Commerce, the State Education Department. The Carson Unified School Board votes to adopt *Carson 3.0* as a policy.

Step 3: Scan the System

Carson conducts a careful analysis of where they are today compared to the vision they dream of. This process, involving surveys of all constituencies as well as learning walk-throughs of all the schools, identifies areas where the reality and the vision are far apart. These gaps will become the focus of the plan for action in the next step.

February of Year 1. Students at the high school respond to the *Carson 3.0 Inventory,* a survey of how the elements of the vision are present in the current situation. Teachers and parents complete similar inventories. The Vision Task Force gathers hard data on which elements of their vision are currently under way and which are missing. They also discuss the vision with focus groups from each constituency.

Each faculty member imagines a *Day in the Life of My Classroom,* specifying how each element of the *Carson 3.0* vision will manifest itself in teaching and learning. As a result, three choose to take early retirement and four seek transfers to other districts. Meanwhile, a flood of experienced and qualified teachers, hearing of Carson's plans, fills the applicant pool. Real estate values rise as families consider moving to Carson.

Superintendent Hunter, accompanied on each visit by a teacher and a student, inventories the Education 3.0 practices in each school in the district. These learning walk-throughs gather further hard evidence of what needs to be done to achieve the *Carson 3.0* vision. As the team walks, they use iPods and iPads to fill out the inventory capture video clips. All these results are sent to the task force, which compiles them into a needs analysis.

March of Year 1. Superintendent Hunter and the principals study the teachers' *Day in the Life* stories, and review the various survey and walk-through results. They identify, at each school, the gaps between current practices and the vision of *Carson 3.0*. From this process, they develop two lists for the district: one of educational needs and another of technical needs.

Step 4: Plan for Action

Faculty and leaders throughout the district work with each other and with outside experts to develop concrete and detailed plans to close each gap identified in the scan of the system. The plan describes educational infrastructure as well as the technical infrastructure that will need to be built, with cost estimates for each piece. Like the vision document, the plan is published in several formats for ease of digestion by the various constituents.

April of Year 1. The leadership team sets a schedule for closing the gaps, both educational and technical. For each item, they set a completion date, name the person responsible for its accomplishment, and estimate a cost. The goal is to introduce the key elements of *Carson 3.0* at the opening of school in September of Year 2, and complete the implementation by the end of the 3rd academic year since the process started.

Faculty members work with a consultant to plan the changes necessary to curriculum, policies, scheduling, and teaching called for by *Carson 3.0*. The technical staff does the same for their part of the new infrastructure, with the consultation of a corporate partner. Both educators and technical people visit other schools that have adopted some of the new practices.

May of Year 1. The work of the leadership team, the faculty, and the technical staff is summarized and published as a podcast, a booklet, and a web page. The costs to build the educational and technical infrastructures are detailed in this plan, and will necessitate a bond issue or tax levy override at Carson Unified. Members of the Vision Task Force, as well as others in the leadership and the community, take the document *Building Carson 3.0* to their constituencies for discussion.

Step 5: Adopt the Plan

Leaders communicate the plan to to its many constituents and build support in the communities. Earlier communications work with the vision makes this task easier, since the plan is no surprise to those who have seen the vision.

June of Year 1. *Building Carson 3.0* is the hot topic around town. Everyone seems to be talking about it. It calls for a major change in the way students are educated, as well as a substantial commitment of public funds. Supporters answer questions and explain details. Selected members of the VisionTask Force meet with the editorial board of the local newspaper. Supporters appear on local television and radio programs. They speak to the Rotary and Exchange Clubs. They build support among faculty and students. The school board arranges finance options with local banks, and seeks state and local grants and matches to help defray the costs.

July of Year 1. The vote for a bond issue and tax levy override succeeds, but the building of public support does not end. The real work of transformation is just beginning for Carson Unified, its teachers, its students, and its leadership.

Step 6: Build Education 3.0

The district Invests in the technical and educational infrastructures necessary to support the vision set forth in the *Day in the Life*. Work focuses on developing the ability of faculty, students, and staff to teach and learn in new ways.

September–December of Year 2. *Building Carson 3.0* in all its detail is posted online as a graphic chart so that all can follow its progress. Accomplishments are posted as they occur. Superintendent Hunter hires a Clerk of the Works for each of the infrastructures, educational and technical. Contracts are let as necessary. A *Carson 3.0* Transformation Task Force meets weekly via WebEx to track progress and solve problems as they occur.

The technical infrastructure for *Carson 3.0* is installed and tested. Wireless, cables, servers, software, learning management system, online curriculum content, student and teacher databases, all are set up and tried out through the network. Tests are conducted with video conferencing, mobile devices, off-site access, and other aspects of the technical infrastructure.

Mr. Bacon, the science teacher, and his faculty colleagues get laptops, iPads, video cameras, data probes, and other technologies necessary to their transformation objectives. Each writes a personal teaching, learning, and technology professional development plan, based on the *Day in the Life* story they each wrote earlier in the process. Each gets a coach to help them work through it.

September–August of Year 2. Faculty plan a year of work for their students: courses, units, and group projects, all carefully coordinated with each other. They also familiarize themselves with their technical infrastructure, their online curriculum content, and their new digital devices. The collective bargaining agreement is modified to enable the working conditions for faculty called for in *Carson 3.0*.

September of Year 3. School opens under a new organizational scheme and some very different practices in teaching and learning.

Step 7: Monitor and Refresh

The district tracks its progress through the plan of action, and its accomplishment of the principles of its vision, through a variety of channels. After the 1st year of implementation, it will refresh its vision and adopt a plan of action for the 2nd year.

September–June of Year 3. As the first year of *Carson 3.0* progresses, the Transformation Task Force keeps its fingers on the pulses of transformation. They conduct quarterly surveys of students, faculty, and parents, measuring how well they are approaching the principles set forth in the *Carson 3.0* vision. In addition to these formal measurements, the task force collects comments and suggestions through informal channels as well. They meet monthly to share their findings and take care of difficulties that arise. And they publish quarterly an online progress report to the community.

Another school's experience with the Education 3.0 process may not match exactly that of Carson Unified School District. In fact, every school that has gone through the process has done it differently. The key items of success, and the focus of this book, are a strong vision for a transformed school, viewed through the eyes of a student, and a commitment to invest in the necessary tools and changes to make that vision come true.

Many additional examples from Education 3.0 schools, along with sample presentations, podcasts, and visioning tools, are available at this book's website: www.ed3dot0.net.

CHAPTER 1

Recognize the Need for Change

Most communities are happy with their schools. For them to consider the kind of transformation described in Education 3.0, they will need to question seriously their complacency and come to understand that their schools may not be adequate for the future.

Some communities are disappointed with their schools and are seeking to transform them, but are not sure which direction to take. They need to understand how their schools got that way, and to realize that tinkering at the margins of the current system will not get them the schools they need.

This chapter provides a beginning point for both types of communities, and for those in between. It begins with a brief analysis of how schools have over time adapted to serve the societies around them and how the last 20 years have witnessed a failure to adapt on the part of many schools. Through the eyes of contemporary painters and photographers, it documents how Education 1.0 developed to serve the needs of an agricultural and artisanal society in the 19th century, and how schools adapted to an industrial economy through Education 2.0 in the 20th century. In the end it considers how Education 3.0 should adapt to an information society . . . and invites the reader to paint a picture of a transformed school.

We'll begin with a painter of pictures born almost 200 years ago.

EDUCATION 1-2-3

Winslow Homer learned early in life how to draw and paint, first as an illustrator of sheet music covers, later as a lithographer, and famously as a watercolorist. Born in 1836, he rendered faithfully the life of the times: the sailors and farmers, the war, the storms, the children, and the schools (see Figures 1.1–1.3).

At Work. Homer's life spanned a period of growth and westward movement, but also an era of relative stability in people's lives and work. We see common themes reflected in Winslow Homer's work: people in

FIGURE 1.1. Homer's *Waiting for an Answer.*

FIGURE 1.2. Homer's *Breezing Up.*

FIGURE 1.3. Homer's *Snap the Whip.*

small groups going about their daily routines; their closeness to nature; their spirit manifest in their hands and faces.

Don't you wish sometimes you could live back then? Everything was simpler. You walked to the local school, taught by your neighbor's daughter, worked in the fields or at the shore, and enjoyed the company of a few friends. Some common elements appear in Homer's works:

- People in groups of two or three working and figuring things out together
- Simple hand tools, and very few of them
- People of varied ages in the same setting
- No two people doing exactly the same thing
- A range of clothing colors and styles
- A clear view of the world outside
- A small circle of interaction and interdependency

At School. Let's take a closer look, through Homer's work, at the school of those halcyon days (see Figure 1.4). What do we see?

- People in groups of two or three working and figuring things out together; simple hand tools, and very few of them; people of varied ages in the same setting; no two people doing exactly the same thing—and so on.

FIGURE 1.4. Homer's *Country School.*

The schools of this era reflect their adaptation to the world around them. Life in school, and life outside, were pretty much the same. The school reflected the society it served. Children in school learned what they needed to survive and succeed in the world outside. The way you worked at school, the tools you used, the schedule you kept, and the circle you moved in, fit well into the agricultural and artisanal economy of the day.

Education 1.0

Winslow Homer painted in the era of Education 1.0, when schools were designed to prepare farmers and craftsmen and weavers and cooks, who worked with simple hand tools in an economic and social environment that remained static for four and five decades at a time. In this first phase of American school history, schools settled into a comfortable pattern of preparing young people for pastoral prosperity.

As you consider this comfortable harmony, ask yourself this question—a question that we will repeat several times as we move through the seven steps of transformation: Which of the following was the most important thing for young people to learn in this era?

- Reading, writing, and arithmetic?
- To be on time, to follow directions, and to get your work done?
- To be curious and creative?

- Collaborative problem solving with a small group?
- History, the sciences, and literature?

Then consider the student's perspective. As you look at Homer's paintings of young people, ask yourself these questions:

- What's on their minds?
- What's in their hands?
- What do they hope for?

The success of your school's transformation to Education 3.0 will depend on how thoroughly you wrestle with these questions at each step in the process.

Education 2.0

At Work. By the year of Homer's death, 1910, society had changed. More and more people worked in the factory, in the office, on the line, rather than on the farm, in the kitchen, and in the field. Let's take a look at some photographs of the workplaces of the early 20th century, taken between 1910 and 1930 (see Figures 1.5–1.7).

The world of work documented here has come a long way from the farms and fields of Homer's paintings. What do we see in these photographs?

- People working alone at an individual work station
- Specialized mechanical tools, one for each person
- People of about the same age in each setting
- Most people doing exactly the same thing as the person next to them
- A uniformity of clothing styles and colors
- Little or no connection with the world outside

We might call this "Workplace 2.0."

This visual evidence of change in the workplace is corroborated by statistical measures, as shown in Table 1.1.

At School. Now let's take a look at the schools of the same era, again through photography (see Figures 1.8 and 1.9). What do we see? People working alone at an individual desk, specialized mechanical tools, one for each person, people of about the same age in each setting, most people doing exactly the same thing as the person next to them, and so on. As

FIGURE 1.5. Cigar Factory Workers in Ybor City, Florida.

FIGURE 1.6. Boot Factory Workers in Carlow, Ireland.

FIGURE 1.7. Office Workers at Desks.

TABLE 1.1. Occupational Structure of the United States, 1870–2000.

	Percent of the Labor Force							
	1870	*1900*	*1930*	*1950*	*1972*	*1972**	*1990*	*2000*
Occupation:								
Professionals and technicians	3	4	7	9	14	13	17	19
Managers, officials, and proprietors	6	6	7	9	10	9	13	15
Sales workers	{ 4	5	6	7	7	10	12	13
Clerical workers	{	3	9	12	17	16	15	14
Craftsmen and foremen	9	11	13	14	13	13	12	12
Operatives	10	13	16	20	17	16	11	9
Laborers, except farm	9	12	11	7	5	6	4	4
Service workers	6	9	10	10	13	13	13	12
Farmers and farm laborers	53	38	21	12	3	5	3	3
Total	100	100	100	100	100	100	100	100
Number in labor force (millions)	12.9	29.0	48.7	59.0	81.7	82.1	117.9	136.2
Percent of labor force female	15	18	22	28	38	38	45	47

SOURCES: 1870 from Edwards 1943; 1900–1950 from U.S. Census Bureau 1975; 1972 from U.S. Census Bureau, *Statistical Abstract of the United States*: 1973, and U.S. Department of Labor, *Employment and Earnings*, January 1984; 1990 and 2000 from U.S. Department of Labor, *Employment and Earnings*, January 1991 and 2001b.

*The last three columns, based on the 1980 Census classification of occupations, are not directly comparable with the first five, which are consistent with the 1970 Census classification.

FIGURE 1.8. Schoolroom in Duryea, Pennsylvania.

the 20th century began, our schools were no longer as sleepy and sylvan. They woke to the challenge of industrialization, and the nature of the school changed. Schools shifted their paradigm to prepare people to survive and succeed in the industrial workplace. They entered the era of Education 2.0.

What were the most important things for young people to learn for Workplace 2.0?

- Reading, writing, and arithmetic?
- To be on time, to follow directions, and to get your work done?
- Curiosity and creativity?
- Collaborative problem solving with a small group?
- History, the sciences, and literature?

And now consider the student's perspective. As you look at the photographs of young people in Education 2.0, ask yourself:

- What's on their minds?
- What's in their hands?
- What do they hope for?

FIGURE 1.9. Schoolroom in Richland, Ohio.

Table 1.2 reviews the story so far, a comparison of the key elments of the two major eras of schooling, Education 1.0 and Education 2.0.

Education 3.0?

At Work. Now we'll jump ahead a century. One hundred years after Workplace 2.0—that's today—let's examine, again through photography, what the world of work looks like (see Figures 1.10–1.12).

What do we see?

- People working in small groups to solve new problems
- Digital information tools on the desktop and in their hands
- Few people doing exactly the same thing as the person next to them
- A variety of ages working together in the same setting
- A diversity of colors and styles of people working together
- A variety of tasks and groupings

TABLE 1.2. A Comparison of the Features of Education 1.0 and Education 2.0

Education 1.0	Education 2.0
Agriculture, artisanry	Manufacturing, processing.
Cooperative small-group work	Solitary work in a group setting
Variety of tasks	Repetitive tasks
Hand tools	Mechanical tools

FIGURE 1.10. Office Workers Around a Computer.

These pictures represent Workplace 3.0, the information age doing its business in this 21st century of ours.

At School. Now, if the schools have been keeping up with the changes in society, we would expect them to reflect this new world of work. We would expect Education 3.0 to prepare people for this new workplace. So let's take our camera into the schools of today (Figures 1.13–1.15). What do we see?

Could photos similar to these be taken in your school today? In these images, we see

- People working alone at an individual desk
- Specialized mechanical tools (the pencil and paper), one for each person

FIGURE 1.11. Laboratory with Instrumentation.

FIGURE 1.12. Power Plant Control Room.

FIGURE 1.13. Middle School Students in Classroom.

- People of about the same age in each setting
- Most people doing exactly the same thing as the person next to them
- A uniformity of styles and colors of people and work
- Little or no connection with the world outside

Will these students be prepared to survive and succeed in the modern workplace? Will they know how to use the information tools necessary to compete in a knowledge-based economy? How different are they from the photographs of Education 2.0?

These photos raise questions for the educators of today:

- What should Education 3.0 look like?
- What should students learn to prepare them for Workplace 3.0?
- How should they learn it?
- How should teachers teach in Education 3.0?
- What tools should they be using for their work?
- Is my school in stage 2.0 or 3.0?
- If you could hire Winslow Homer today to paint a picture of your ideal school to illustrate Education 3.0, what would be in the picture?

FIGURE 1.14. Elementary School Students with Books at Desks.

FIGURE 1.15. High School Students Taking Tests.

This chapter helps you recognize the need for change in the schools, your own and all the rest. The remainder of this book helps you think through the nature of Education 3.0, and shows you how to build it in your schools. But first we step aside for a moment to ask *why:*

- Why are schools today slow to adapt themselves to the world around them?
- Why is it taking so long for them to adopt obviously useful technologies?

Our answers come in the form of two case studies and an analysis of lag time.

BOATS AND CHEESE

The section above, "Education 1-2-3," illustrated the changing nature of the workplace and the role of technology in it. It showed an American economy that has shifted quickly from manufacturing to information, from making things to moving ideas. And it essentiallywarned the next generation not to prepare themselves for work in a factory that no longer exists.

But we still have factories, and they employ millions of workers. In the United States we don't make many refrigerators or computers or televisions anymore; these are manufactured for the most part overseas. But we still make high-tech articles such as aircraft and automobiles, and low-tech items such as boats and cheese. Let's visit two plants that manufacture the last two items, to see the kinds of jobs and the kinds of technologies that exist in those workplaces—and to consider the implications for how we should plan for Education 3.0.

Boats

The TPI factory in Warren, Rhode Island, has been making boats for more than 50 years. In the middle of the sprawling factory floor are hulls in various stages of assembly, some empty shells, others ready to roll out the door to the launch ramp. From a small sailboat that Stuart Little would find familiar to larger cruisers being built for the U.S. Navy, the array represents the range of current boat production.

A boat is assembled from hundreds of parts, each manufactured in one of the shops that surround the main factory floor. One shop makes the hull, another the deck, others construct the floors, walls, and teak trim

FIGURE 1.16. Robot Machine.

pieces. All are highly automated. What strikes the visitor is the lack of people—and the lack of noise. No banging, no yelling, no muscle work. The few workers in the plant are wearing blue button-down shirts and electronic ID tags. Their hands rest on computer keyboards more than on wrenches or screwdrivers. The soft hum of machinery and exhaust fans seem to quiet the place down.

Today's boat is a precision instrument, crafted for speed, strength, durability, and light weight. Its parts are created not by people at lathes but by computer-controlled robots. Look at Figure 1.16. Where's the worker? He's standing several feet away, safely monitoring the action. His hands are folded, his shirt spotless, his mind focused on how he might speed up or improve the manufacturing process. What skills does he need to succeed at this work? Will he learn them at your school?

Cheese

We import very little cheese from China. It's one of the few things that we still make at home. At the Cabot Farmer's Cooperative factory in the

FIGURE 1.17. Technician in Cheese Factory.

hills of rural Vermont, millions of pounds of cheddar go out the door each year aboard trucks bound for every state in the union. At the other end of the plant, huge pipes funnel in millions of gallons of milk from New England cows. In between we can see the cheese-making process, a natural organic transformation that humans have employed for thousands of years: Expose the milk to the air, add a little acid, watch the temperature, and wait for the curds to form. Then compress the solids, let it age, and finally slice it onto your sandwich.

On the factory floor, you might expect to see a team of wrinkled codgers in plaid shirts and overalls stirring the pots, turning the valves, and tasting the samples. But they are nowhere to be found. Instead, the visitor sees scientists in white lab coats armed with test tubes and computers (see Figure 1.17). While they monitor the process in the lab, the machines that make the cheese are run by computers.

Not too many jobs in this factory can be filled by unskilled workers, or by those limited to carrying out routine tasks. The routine tasks are done by the machines. The workers are there to program the machines, monitor them with precision, solve problems when they go wrong, and design new machines that make the cheese better. Are the students at your school learning what they need to carry out these kinds of tasks?

FIGURE 1.18. Graph of Skills.

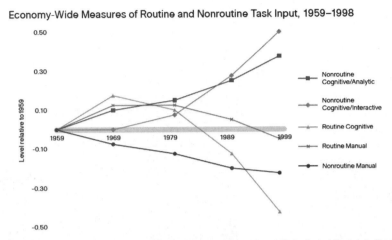

Economy-Wide Measures of Routine and Nonroutine Task Input, 1959–1998

From: Autor, D., Levy, F. and Murnane, R. (2001) "The Skill Content of Recent Technological Change: An Empirical Exploration." NBER Working Paper 8337. Boston, MA: National Bureau of Economic Research.

THE SKILLS WE NEED

Boats and cheese are real, substantive physical entities that are still manufactured by Americans. They are neither digital, nor informational, nor service products. They are part of the old economy. But today they are made in new ways that call for a set of skills that were not so important in the old economy. These include problem solving, numerical analysis, engineering design, applied chemistry, statistics, and close observation. And these skills are required for the lowest level workers in the system; their supervisors must possess all these and more.

If basic products like boats and cheese require this level of technical skill and intellectual understanding, imagine what is required to manufacture more complex items. The expectations and standards of yesterday will not suffice for the world our students will move into.

Nonroutine Cognitive/Analytic

The subheading above comes from a research paper in the *Quarterly Journal of Economics*. According to the authors, it describes a new type of skill, one that we think has a lot to do with Education 3.0. In "The Skill Content of Recent Technological Change: An Empirical Exploration," D. H. Autor, F. Levy, and R. J. Murnane define *nonroutine cognitive tasks* as "tasks demanding flexibility, creativity, generalized problem-solving and complex communications." The three economists who conducted the research studied the kinds of tasks that workers faced in the workplace, starting in the 1950s, and running right up through the 21st century. They found that the kinds of tasks have been shifting, away from routine manual tasks (down steadily since 1960) and routine cognitive tasks (up until 1970, then down ever since) and toward nonroutine analytic (steeply rising since 1980) and nonroutine interactive tasks (rising even steeper since 1990). Their data are gathered from U.S. Department of Labor surveys.[1]

The authors explain that the routine tasks have left the human workplace, and are now being done by machines and computers. They point to several occupations that have disappeared or changed radically during this period:

> To provide one example, the 1976 edition of the Department of Labor's *Occupation Outlook Handbook* described the job of Secretary as: ". . . Secretaries relieve their employers of routine duties so they can work on more important matters. Although most secretaries type, take shorthand, and deal with callers, the time spent on these duties varies in different types of organizations" (U. S. Department of Labor 1976, p. 94). In 2000 the entry for "Secretary" reads:
>
> As technology continues to expand in of.ces across the Nation, the role of the secretary has greatly evolved. Office automation and organizational restructuring have led secretaries to assume a wide range of new responsibilities once reserved for managerial and professional staff. Many secretaries now provide training and orientation to new staff, conduct research on the Internet, and learn to operate new office technologies. (p. 324)[2]

What does this have to do with Education 3.0? For one thing, it means we shouldn't use new technologies such as computers simply to teach the times tables or home row keys more efficiently. Not much future there. If we use our new technology to teach these kinds of routine cognitive skills, we are not preparing our students for the workplace, or for college. Instead, we should use the technology to teach the skills that will be in high demand—what the researchers call "nonroutine cognitive, analytic, and interactive skills," the skills needed for the rising tide of tasks in the workplace. (By *interactive skills*, they mean those calling for communication and interaction with other people.) What do these skills look like?

A recent white paper on education from Cisco Systems answers this question very directly. An excerpt follows:

A New Set of Skills

The citizens of the 21st century need to supplement their foundational skills and knowledge with a new set of skills that are in much higher demand than before. There is much debate about these "21st century skills," but though the exact categories may differ, these eight groupings are consistently identified:

- Gathering, synthesizing, and analyzing information.
- Working autonomously to a high standard with minimal supervision.
- Leading other autonomous workers through influence.
- Being creative and turning that creativity into action.
- Thinking critically and asking the right questions.
- Striving to understand others' perspectives and to understand the entirety of an issue.
- Communicating effectively, often using technology.
- Working ethically, firmly based in both your own society and the planet as a whole.[3]

Global companies with American roots, such as Cisco and Apple, understand that our economy will not thrive without constant invention and innovation, and that we need to develop a workforce capable of these tasks. The workforce that served us well in the industrial age is not what we need right now.

A middle-class lifestyle in the United States calls for a wage of $30 an hour plus benefits.[4] Well-educated, experienced workers in China, with excellent routine cognitive skills, will work for $5 an hour. If we want to earn $30 per hour in the global economy, we need to invent, innovate, and practice nonroutine analytical skills, and do it better than the rest of the world—much better. That's the only hope for our economy. This point of view is echoed in a 2011 Harvard Business School study of 5,000 successful companies and innovators. J. H. Dyer, H. B. Gregersen, and C. M. Christensen found that those who thrive in the new economy share a set of discovery skills that distinguish them from the rest:

Observing. "Most innovators are intense observers. They carefully watch the world around them, and as they observe how things work, they often become sensitized to what doesn't work. . . . As they engage in these types of observations, they begin to connect common threads across unconnected data, which may provoke uncommon business ideas. Such observations often engage multiple senses and are frequently prompted by compelling questions."

Questioning. "Innovators are consummate questioners who show a passion for inquiry. Their queries frequently challenge the status quo, just as [Steve] Jobs did when he asked, "Why does a computer need a fan?" . . . Innovators, like Jobs, ask questions to understand how things really are today, why they are that way, and how they might be changed or disrupted."

Associating. "Associating happens as the brain tries to synthesize and make sense of novel inputs. It helps innovators discover new directions by making connections across seemingly unrelated questions, problems, or ideas."

Networking. "Innovators spend a lot of time and energy finding and testing ideas through a diverse network of individuals who vary wildly in their backgrounds and perspectives . . . They actively search for new ideas by talking to people who may offer a radically different view of things."

Experimenting. "Innovators are constantly trying out new experiences and piloting new ideas. Experimenters unceasingly explore the world intellectually and experientially, holding convictions at bay and testing hypotheses along the way."[5]

When you read in the next chapter the *Day in the Life of Sally,* a high school student, ask yourself if she exhibits these five key modes of discovery. Ask also if Sally's day develops the kinds of deeper learning called for by the National Academies of Science in their 2012 report, *Education for Life and Work: Developing Transferable Knowledge and Skills in the 21st Century.*[6]

We define "deeper learning" as the process through which an individual becomes capable of taking what was learned in one situation and applying it to new situations (i.e., transfer). Through deeper learning (which often involves shared learning and interactions with others in a community), the individual develops expertise in a particular domain of knowledge and/or performance. The product of deeper learning is transferable knowledge, including content knowledge in a domain and knowledge of how, why, and when to apply this knowledge to answer questions and solve problems. We refer to this blend of both knowledge and skills as "21st-century competencies." The competencies are structured around fundamental principles of the content area and their relationships rather than disparate, superficial facts or procedures. It is the way in which the individual and community structures and organizes the intertwined knowledge and skills—rather than the separate facts or procedures per se—that supports transfer. While other types of learning may allow an individual to recall facts, concepts, or procedures, deeper learning allows the individual to transfer what was learned to solve new problems.

The demand for higher level skills is rising rapidly; for routine skills the demand is falling fast. Even the mundane tasks of building boats and making cheese call for more of the former than the latter. And so your vision for Education 3.0 must consider this reality.

LAG TIME

Why haven't today's schools adapted to the needs of the society around them, shifted toward a new set of skills, and adopted the useful technologies invented by the information age?

Over 150 years ago, Henry David Thoreau asked the same question. He complained that his courses at Harvard were devoid of practical application, and not updated to match the progress of science and the arts. Of his course in navigation at Harvard College, he remarked, "Why, if I had taken one turn down the harbor I should have known more about it."[7] He concluded that learning "should not be one thing in the schoolroom, and another in the street." He longed for a clearer reflection of the world outside to find its way into the academy.[8]

The lag time in the adoption of new technologies by schools is nothing new. Schools by their nature are slow to adapt to the world around them and adopt new tools and methods that can support their mission. The book, invented in the days of Gutenberg (d. 1468), and mass-produced on a wide scale 150 years later, was not widely adopted by American schools until 1850, with the rise of the McGuffey readers.[9] Other fields such as medicine and law adopted the very useful technology of the book in half the time. A similar lag time occurs in the adoption of the machine-made pencil, invented in 1825, mass-produced 50 years later, and widely adopted in the trades and business by 1875. Not until after the First World War did pencils begin to replace inkwells and nibs in schools—a full century after their invention.[10] Both of these technologies offered clear advantages to the schools' mission, but took twice as long to arrive.

Examples

The lag time among invention, mass production, and ubiquity of new technologies has been getting shorter over the years. Table 1.3 illustrates six information technologies that have found their ways into our lives over the last 500 years. Notice that in each case, the new technology takes twice as long to become commonplace in schools.

TABLE 1.3. New Technology Lag Time

Item	Invention	Full Adoption by industry	Lag time	Full Adoption by schools	Lag time
Book	1450	1700	250	1850	400
Pencil	1825	1875	50	1925	100
Radio	1910	1940	30	Not yet	100+
Television	1945	1965	20	Not yet	60+
Computer	1985	2000	15	Not yet	25+
Mobile phone	1990	2000	10	Not yet	20+

Explanations

Why does it take schools twice as long to adapt and adopt such evidently useful methods and technologies? Here are some possible reasons:

- Schools' implicit mission is to transmit the previous culture to the next generation, not to prepare them for a new culture.
- Schools draw the most conservative, risk-averse people to their ranks.
- School people tend to go from school to college and back to school again, seldom spending time in the world outside where they might observe the technological changes taking place.
- Schools' diverse and public governance makes transformative decisions difficult to take.
- Schools' purpose is custodial and pacifying; new technologies are often disruptive to this end.
- Schools' compulsory nature and public monopoly prevent market forces from forcing adaptation.
- The new technologies often threaten the power base of the people who run the schools.
- Schools lack the extra funds necessary to invest in new ways of doing things.

Of course, all of these explanations contribute to the lag time. These explanations applied in Thoreau's time as they do now, and none of them is insurmountable. The case studies in this book will show many examples of educators who have overcome these forces to build islands of Education 3.0.

Thoreau's father ran a pencil factory. Henry David was an early adopter of pencil technology, taking it with him to Walden Pond and down the

Concord and Merrimack rivers and along the beaches of Cape Cod. The portable pencil—a 19th-century mobile learning device—enabled him to write as he took his turns down the harbors and made his observations in the fields. With one foot in the academy and another in the street, Thoreau was able to transcend both worlds. Thoreau recognized the need for change and acted on it. He serves as a model for many of today's educators who are adapting their schools to Education 3.0.

In the next chapter we'll visit a student who has outgrown her pencils. If schools are slow to transform themselves into version 3.0, perhaps it's because they lack a clear vision of what school could look like if it took full advantage of 21st-century learning devices. The next chapter helps you paint this vision as seen through the eyes of your students.

CHAPTER 2

Set the Vision

Your task at this step is to paint a picture of what Education 3.0 should look like at your school, and in your community. As you paint, you'll want to make sure that you consider two worlds:

- The world outside of the school, Workplace 3.0, that we saw illustrated in the previous chapter.
- The world inside the student's mind and body, full of energy and craving accomplishment.

Your vision of Education 3.0 should also illustrate the new forms of teaching and learning, the updated curriculum, the revised policies, and the central role of network technologies called for by Workplace 3.0. To help you through this process, this chapter provides you with sample visions drawn from schools that have gone through the seven-step process of transformation, and a summary of the key principles they have developed. But don't let these models influence you too much. It's your own brainstorming and imagination that are your best guides to your own vision.

In this chapter, you will examine the visions developed by other schools, review the key principles of Education 3.0, develop a list of key ideas and illustrative examples that you want to include in your own vision, and create a multimedia description of a *Day in the Life of a Student* at your transformed school.

The best visions are built by a team of educators, working with parents, school board members, and businesspeople. As you paint the picture of your transformed school, each member of the team wields his or her own paintbrush. This can get messy. And the result will please no one unless you all talk about the outlines of the painting before you start and agree on the underlying sketch.

The result of this step of the process is a multimedia presentation of a *Day in the Life of a Student*. You'll also publish a written description of this student's day, all suitable for communication with students, parents, faculty, and the other members of the school community whose support you'll need to accomplish the transformation.

We'll take our first glimpse of Education 3.0 through the eyes of a student we'll call Sally. The student is the focus of our educational efforts; what happens to the student in the course of a day determines in large measure what and how well the student learns. So we'll begin our journey toward Education 3.0 by following Sally through a day of work. *This Day in the Life of a Student* or *Day in the Life of Sally* is a compilation drawn from the dreams developed by six of the high schools listed in the preface.

As you consider Sally's day, think back to Winslow Homer's painting of the country school in Chapter 1. Contrast Sally's day in Education 3.0 with that of one of the students in the old painting. And contrast the world you see through the windows of Homer's schoolroom with the world that Sally will enter when she finishes school.

A DAY IN THE LIFE OF A STUDENT

For the purposes of this chapter, we'll consider our student to be enrolled at a technologically advanced school called H.S. 21+. We'll follow Sally through a day of schoolwork, a day designed especially to illustrate the principles of Education 3.0.

6:30 a.m. Sally wakes to the ping of an instant message (IM) arriving on her mobile device. It's from another student at H.S. 21+ who is working with her on an environmental chemistry project.

> Schoolwork starts early for our hypothetical student, because 180 days times 6 hours per day is not sufficient to develop the skills and talents necessary for success in the 21st century. And new communication technologies, such as instant messaging, allow students to be connected with their schoolwork and their colleagues all day, every day.

6:35 a.m. Sally researches, from her laptop, the various laws and guidelines on allowable concentrations of PCBs in drinking water. She finds that the U.S. Environmental Protection Agency has set the Maximum Contaminant Level at 0.5 parts per billion.

> From her teachers and librarians, our student has learned how to search effectively the online sources that are increasingly available to her, how to determine the authority and reliability of a source, and how to skim the search results to find the germ of truth that she seeks.

6:40 a.m. Sally checks the readings from the probe at the city drinking water monitoring station, which has recently been connected to a web server, so that she can see the readings in real time.

> Real-time data from all over the world is increasingly available to anyone who can connect to the right web page. The curriculum at H.S. 21+ is designed to take advantage of this, and to develop student skill in using it.

6:50 a.m. Sally sends an instant message to the members of her project group, explaining that she saw concentrations of PCBs of 0.7 and 0.8 ppb at times over the last 24 hours. She attaches a graph of the ups and downs, that she constructed with the spreadsheet program on her laptop.

> Our student is a member of a collaborative project group, assigned by her teachers to come up with a solution to an issue of public interest as well as academic importance. The kinds of problems they get, and the ways they work on them, are similar to those in the 21st-century world of work.

6:55 a.m. Sally sends a short report of her findings, with attached data, sources, and graph, to her personal online academic portfolio on the school's web server.

> Student work at H.S. 21+ is seldom handed in on paper. Rather, it's kept by each student in an online portfolio, a collection of work that provides evidence of learning to their teachers and might later be used for admission to college or an interview for a job.

7:00 a.m. After practicing her violin, Sally breakfasts with her mom and dad. She is careful not to drink any water from the tap.

> At meals, the family often discusses the ideas our student encounters at school. In fact, the school provides on its web site family discussion questions that tie into the curriculum.

7:30 a.m. On the subway on the way to school Sally listens to a podcast of last week's debate in the state senate on the clean water bill, that she downloaded from the school server.

> H.S. 21+ takes advantage of the information devices that students carry in their pockets, by developing and collecting educational

podcasts that provide background and extension to the core curriculum materials.

7:40 a.m. The subway is delayed, so Sally has time to read, from the same iPod, the next chapter of Thoreau's *Walden* for English class. She downloaded this and many other readings from the school server.

The school provides an extensive library of electronic texts that can be downloaded to students' laptops or to their iPods.

7:55 a.m. At the school library Sally meets with two other members of her project group to discuss what they've found over the last two days, and what they need to do next. She learns that the PCB limit in the Senate bill is set at 0.7 ppb.

The library at H.S. 21+ is no longer just a place to store books—it's become the hub of the school, with spaces designed especially to facilitate the small-group project meetings that have become an important mode of learning at the school.

8:10 a.m. In a large-group math class in the small auditorium, Sally learns about statistical sampling techniques in environmental analysis from a scientist at the EPA in Washington who appears through a WebEx connection.

Desktop video conferencing capabilities turn any computer at H.S. 21+ into a distance-learning station. Subject matter experts, guest speakers, and remote teachers make regular appearances in classrooms and at worktables, extending the human resources available to students as they learn.

8:20 a.m. Sally realizes that her data gathering from the online probe might not be accurate, because of the small number of sample readings she collected. She questions the scientist in real time over the WebEx connection.

The statistics concepts our student learns in math class are especially designed to coordinate with the topics and assignments of the science curriculum; it's not by happenstance that our student's small-group project task requires data sampling and conclusion making that calls for certain mathematical understandings.

8:30 a.m. From the auditorium, Sally reexamines the data in her spreadsheet with one of her colleagues who is still in the library, sharing their screens to compare their findings. She begins to rethink her conclusions.

> Students at H.S. 21+ are encouraged to stay in touch with each other and with online resources, even while they are engaged in a lecture or presentation. In fact, the faculty rewards students who interrupt the class with ideas and resources from the outside.

9:20 a.m. Sally sends an instant message to a local senate staff intern, double-checking on allowable concentrations of PCB in the latest version of the clean water bill.

> Students at H.S. 21+ use the same communication tools that are used in business, government, and higher education, enabling them at any time to tap into community resources that are relevant to their schoolwork.

9:55 a.m. Math class begins. Sally asks a question about sampling rates in measurement statistics. The math teacher connects to the online water quality probe, copies the data into a spreadsheet, and uses the SmartBoard to show the class how to perform a simple test of significance. Sally copies the formulas to her laptop.

> The math curriculum at H.S. 21+ has shifted toward the kinds of math actually used in science, business, and engineering, such as probability and statistics. It also integrates common software tools and presentation devices, moving away from pencil and paper. Most important, it welcomes coordination with the team projects that drive students' work.

11:00 a.m. The English class discusses the chapter of *Walden* they read last night. The teacher brings up a topographical map of the pond area from Google Earth. Following along on her laptop, Sally switches to a satellite view, and notices a factory very near the pond.

> A theme for this semester at H.S. 21+ is the relationship between humans and their environment, and even the English department goes along.

11:30 a.m. Sally uses Facebook to locate a student at a school near Walden Pond who's interested in environmental science. She sends a note suggesting a collaborative project to measure PCB levels in the pond.

> H.S. 21+ prides itself on developing students who are self-starters and resourceful researchers, who use whatever tools are necessary to get the job done and who identify opportunities to extend their studies in new directions.

11:55 a.m.. At lunch, Sally's project colleague Xu En-lai connects to the web site of *China Daily*. He translates for the others at the table the fact that they are considering a guideline for a 0.6 ppb limit on PCBs in drinking water.

> The online environment at H.S. 21+ encourages access to multilingual and multicultural resources and connections and encourages students to apply them to their projects.

12:30 p.m.. Sally finds the chemistry teacher in the lab learning to use some new probes and software. She asks to learn more about PCBs: what they are, where they come from, and why they are harmful.

> Teachers as well as students are learners at H.S. 21+. Faculty members actively seek out the latest developments in their fields and learn how to use them.

12:35 p.m. The chemistry teacher suggests a self-paced online course on the EPA's web site, which helps Sally and her group better understand the scientific and social issues.

> Each department at H.S. 21+ has assembled a directory of online courses and tutorials relevant to their field, to which they send students.

1:25 p.m. Sally and her team report to their faculty project coach on their progress. He reminds them to save a daily progress report to their academic portfolios and suggests they focus their study on a single aspect of the proposed clean water bill.

> To bring the disparate areas of the curriculum together, to make learning more relevant to the world around them, and to develop

collaboration skills, H.S. 21+ schedules each student into a team project group with a faculty coach, with time allotted for them to work together during the school day. The topics for the team projects are carefully concocted by the faculty to enable contributions from all departments and to aim at problems and issues in the real world.

1:45 p.m. Sally connects to the city's online water quality probe and downloads a much larger sample of readings into her spreadsheet. After applying the statistical tests she learned earlier, she is less sure that the PCB level is dangerous.

Students in the H.S. 21+ apply the basic productivity software tools to what they are studying. Their teachers seek out opportunities for them to practice these tools.

1:55 p.m. Sally also notices a pattern to this longer string of data points—it seems to rise and fall over time. She plots it on her spreadsheet. The faculty coach suggests she try fitting a curve to the data, and shows her how. It is close to a sine curve, with a period of about 6 hours.

The faculty at H.S. 21+ is prepared to deliver just-in-time learning: When a situation arises that demands the application of a new skill or concept, the teacher is ready to teach it. The role of faculty coach to the project groups provides many opportunities for this kind of learning.

2:20 p.m. Three members of the project team meet in the library during their study period. This will be their last face-to-face meeting before tomorrow's presentation of their findings. They discuss the periodic nature of the PCB levels, and realize it times perfectly with the rise and fall of the tide: The PCB levels rise as the tide falls.

Students at H.S. 21+ know they will be rewarded for discovering new patterns and relationships so they actively seek them out. And the school is designed to provide spaces and scheduled time for students to work together to make these discoveries.

2:30 p.m. The team assigns tasks among themselves: One will go down to the riverside to capture video of the tide; another will animate the spreadsheet with the sine curve; Sally will record some introductory music from her violin; another agrees to assemble all these pieces into a multimedia podcast, which will constitute the team's report of their work.

H.S. 21+ supports students' application of images, video, music, and animation to their work whenever they contribute to the understanding of the topic. And they provide a lending library of devices that make media capture and editing and display possible.

3:00 p.m. At basketball practice, Sally talks with her scrimmage partner, who is doing an internship at the local office of the state senator. The clean water bill is in her committee. Sally explains her group's findings, and promises to send a copy of their podcast tonight as soon as it's done.

Sports and community internships are required of all students at H.S. 21+ because they build elements of character that complement academic work.

4:30 p.m. Before leaving school, Sally finds an open practice room and records a bit of Bach on her iPod, which she will later send to the team member who's assembling the podcast. She chooses a piece with a melody that rises and falls, just like the PCB data.

The arts are integrated with the rest of the curriculum. Artistic appreciation, composition, and expression are required for all students, since they have proven themselves to be essential elements of academic and career success.

6:30 p.m. The first draft of the team podcast arrives in her e-mail. Sally sends a draft copy to her friend at the senator's office, and suggests a few corrections to the assembler. Then she's called to supper.

Schoolwork does not end at 3 p.m.. Students are expected to complete much of their academic work after school hours. They don't call it homework, and it seldom consists of problem sets or repetitive exercises—it's mostly work on the group project that happens outside of school.

8:00 p.m. Sally settles in to the novel she's been reading on her eReader.

Students at H.S. 21+ do a lot of reading, not just for schoolwork but for pleasure. Reading fiction may be the best way to confront certain issues and ideas, and Sally's teachers know that reading remains a key skill for success.

8:30 p.m. The ping of an instant message interrupts her reading. Her basketball buddy says the committee wants to play the podcast at the committee meeting, which is still going on, deadlocked on the issue of PCB levels in the clean water bill. Sally gets the rest of her project team in a video chat window, and they all give permission.

> Students at H.S. 21+ learn to use a variety of tools for collaborative work, including video conferencing. This not only builds the kinds of skills they will need to succeed in the future, but enables them to extend their learning beyond the school day.

10:00 p.m. Sally's parents call her in to see the TV news report on the compromise that got the clean water bill out of committee on a 6-4 vote. In the back of the committee room she glimpses a fleeting shot of her animated data plot playing on a senator's iPad.

> Schoolwork takes on a new meaning when it links with what's happening in the world outside of school. Faculty at H.S. 21+ carefully craft the group projects to maximize connection with the important issues of the day.

10:30 p.m. After a short IM chat with her team, Sally is ready for bed. She sleeps contentedly. But she fell asleep wondering—Why would the PCB level vary with the ocean tide?

> The dream of the leadership of H.S. 21+ is to see every student end the day with a sense of wonder and curiosity linked to important academic objectives.

Reflections on A Day in the Life of Sally

Let's reflect on Sally and her day.

- Do you like her?
- Is she heading toward becoming the kind of citizen you'd like her to be?
- How would you describe Sally? Out of control? Self-directed? Free as a bird? Unsupervised? Self-disciplined? Driven to succeed?
- How did she get that way?
- What's on Sally's mind?
- What's in her hands?
- What does she hope for?

- How is her school preparing her for Workplace 3.0?
- How is her day different from a Day in the Life at your school?
- What would need to change at your school to enable the kind of work that Sally does?
- Sally is near the end of her high school career. What did she need to learn in elementary and middle school to prepare her to succeed at H.S. 21+?
- Consider Sally's encounters with her teachers. How would you describe them? How is the role of teachers at your school different from their roles at H.S. 21+?
- What's going on behind the scenes as you watch Sally work through her day? What technologies exist within the walls and on the servers and in her hands? What curriculum preparations had to have been made before Sally woke up in the morning?

Your Vision

The details of Sally's day are drawn from several of the high schools that have gone through the Education 3.0 process. As such, Sally represents a composite that may not be exactly what you will envision at your school. But her story points out the possibilities of a school designed around the future. It also shows the gap between what most of our students experience today, and what they ought to be doing.

Your school needs to invent its own Sally, and take her through a day in her life. Not just her 6 hours at school, but her entire day. Your Sally's day will form the core of your vision, and your authoring of Sally's story—especially the group discussions that lead up to each scene in the day—will uncover the diverse perceptions and dreams of your school community.

Appendix A includes additional Day in the Life stories, at different age levels and with varied emphasis. There's even *a Day in the Life of a Teacher* and a *Day in the Life of a Superintendent*. Read these to inspire your own writing. If you are working with a group, encourage all of the participants to read at least two of the Day in the Life stories before they begin to work on their own.

Most groups that have gone through the Education 3.0 process conduct a serious discussion of the section Education 1-2-3 from the previous chapter and then a no-holds-barred debate about *A Day in the Life of a Student*. This discourse is essential to the process. If you can couple these discussions with visits to schools following the principles of Education 3.0, the planning group will inform itself well for the visioning process that comes next.

PRINCIPLES OF EDUCATION 3.0

We have looked at the history of education in America over the 19th, 20th, and 21st centuries, and glimpsed some Day in the Life stories of Education 3.0 schools. Now we'll delve more deeply into the ideas behind Education 3.0, analyze more closely the Day in the Life stories, and ask you to compare your school with what you have seen. Our goal is to explore these questions:

- What does Education 3.0 look like?
- How is Education 3.0 different from what we are doing today?
- What skills does it focus on? Why?

No two of the dozens of Day in the Life stories that have been developed as part of this process are the same. The diversity of ages, approaches, cultures, and examples is remarkable, drawn as they are from small rural elementary schools to the largest urban high schools in the United States and abroad. But all share a few common themes and ideas, principles that seem to repeat themselves in every community. The Education 3.0 process has uncovered a groundswell of common dreams about what schools should be like, dreams shared by students and school board members, business leaders and teachers, parents and professionals all over the world.

Here are the six principles that occur over and over again and help set Education 3.0 apart:

- Students work on problems worth solving.
- Students and teachers collaborate productively.
- Students engage in self-directed research.
- Students learn how to tell a good story.
- Students employ tools appropriate to the task.
- Students learn to be curious and creative.

Of course students in these schools do many other things as well: They learn their times tables and the causes of the Civil War and play sports and sing in the choir—and master the key ideas of the arts and sciences as described by such groups as the Core Knowledge Foundation. But they accomplish these according to the six key principles of Education 3.0 listed above.

And they use many new technologies as they do this work—but the technology is not at the center of their attention, nor ours. Technology enables many of the things they do, and helps them to work faster and deeper, but it's not an end in itself. Let's look at each principle in turn.

Students Work on Problems Worth Solving

By this we don't mean factoring polynomials, or the other examples of arcane academic problems that seem to fill up most of the time in Education 2.0. Rather, we mean students work on problems the world needs to solve to make it a better place. It might be that one of these problems could require the factoring of a polynomial or two; if so, the students would learn that when they needed it. That's the difference between *just-in-time* learning and *just-in-case* learning. In the Day in the Life stories included in this book, our students do such things as:

- Work with a collaborative project group to solve an issue of public interest as well as academic importance
- Find the concepts in one subject fully coordinated with the topics and assignments of the others
- Learn the aspects of their subjects actually used in the real world, such as probability and statistics, estimation and measurement in math
- Work at a community internship to build elements of character that complement academic work

Students Collaborate Productively

They seldom work alone on a project, but they are often solely responsible for an aspect of the group's work. They take advantage of digital communication tools to collaborate with teachers, distant experts, and peers as they work. The ways they work mirror the ways adults work in modern-day businesses and laboratories. In the Day in the Life stories, our students do the following:

- Work in a credit-bearing team project group with a faculty coach, during time allotted for this purpose within the school day
- Meet with their peers in spaces designed especially to facilitate small-group project work
- Use desktop video conferencing for distance learning, discussions with subject matter experts, guest speakers, or remote teachers
- Discuss with their families the ideas they encounter at school, using the family discussion questions from the school's web site
- Connect to multilingual, multicultural, and international resources, and apply them to their academic projects

Students Engage in Self-Directed Research

Student research is aimed at solving the kinds of problems described above, and is often original and along lines their teachers have never explored. Seldom do students research the same old questions from last year; seldom is the entire class researching the same topic. And always they are gathering ideas from a much wider array of sources, made available through digital archives and networks. When doing their research, students in the Day in the Life stories do some or all of these things:

- Effectively search online sources, determine their authority and reliability, and skim the search results to find what they seek
- Use real-time data from their own digital probes and from sources all over the world to explore issues and solve problems
- Use an extensive library of electronic texts, tutorials, and online courses that they downloaded to their laptops and mobile devices
- Use digital communication technologies to tap the knowledge of peers and online experts
- Complete much of their academic work—especially their independent and group project work—outside of school hours

Students Learn How to Tell a Good Story

Explaining, publishing, presenting, and persuading are important skills for every student in Education 3.0. Throughout their school careers, and throughout each day in their school lives, they are called upon to compose, prepare, and present their ideas through public speaking, slide shows, prose, and podcasts—the same forms used in higher education and business. Students in our model school do the following things:

- Employ images, video, music, and animation to bring deeper understanding to their academic work and presentations
- Borrow from the school's lending library of devices to make media capture and editing and display possible
- Publish their work to an online multimedia portfolio that provides evidence of learning
- Present the results of their work to an audience outside the school, combining oral presentation and digital media

Students Employ Tools Appropriate to the Task

Just as you seldom see pencil and paper employed in modern offices or universities or laboratories, these 18th-century tools are rare in the hands of students at our Education 3.0 school. Instead, they use whatever tool works best for the task at hand: computer, calculator, mobile device, keyboard, or data probe. Students employ technological tools in these ways:

- Use digital communication technologies such as instant messaging to work with teachers, peers, and community
- Listen to podcasts on mobile devices that extend and enhance their academic work
- Use digital tools such as video conferencing, shared documents, and learning management systems to get their work done
- Use digital tools to develop animations, videos, presentations, and podcasts that support their academic work

Students Learn to Be Curious and Creative

At our model schools, curiosity and creativity are not thought of as personality traits but as habits of mind and modes of work that must be taught, practiced, and assessed in all subject areas. Without them, students are less likely to succeed in college and in work and also less likely to enjoy their lives. For these reasons, students in the Day in the Life stories do or experience the following:

- Identify opportunities to extend their studies in new directions, then apply the necessary tools to get the job done
- Are rewarded for discovering new patterns and relationships
- Apply artistic appreciation, composition, and expression to their problem solving and academic work
- Are assigned tasks that expect them to seek out new approaches and design unheard-of solutions
- End the day with a sense of wonder and curiosity linked to important academic objectives

At My School

How many of the students in your classroom did the things listed under the six principles of Education 3.0 today? In your school? In your district? What changes would need to take place to make more of this happen? What technologies would they need?

Take a close look at a student in your school. What's on his mind? What's in his hands? What does he hope for? Is he preparing himself for Workplace 3.0? Is he taking full advantage of the information technologies that can help him learn? Is the school capitalizing on his natural energies and sense of industry? Your consideration of these questions will prepare you to set your own vision for Education 3.0.

SETTING THE VISION

The goal in this step of the process is to have the school community develop in their minds a solid picture of what teaching and learning will look like in their transformed school and publish this vision in a multimedia format that communicates well to teachers, parents and community. This is not as easy as it sounds. People harbor wildly conflicting ideas of what school should look like and use a wide range of vocabularies to describe it. To gain meaningful consensus around a solid vision takes time and energy and lots of work.

The group will be creating not a white paper or a policy statement, but a slide show. This sequence of images will follow a student through a typical day at the transformed school, illustrating the key elements of the district's vision. Throughout the process, they'll be using images to communicate what they mean, and then later narrating the images with their voices. This seemingly backward process has proven itself to be a very productive and creative way to set a vision.

There are five activities in this step:

1. *Key ideas and illustrations*, where the school community proposes and discusses the key elements of their transformed schools and suggests concrete illustrations of each one
2. *Sketches*, where the community, working in small groups, draws— with pencil on paper or on their iPads—scenes from a proposed Day in the Life of their student, then presents and discusses them with colleagues
3. *Scripts*, where the community writes for each sketch an explanation, from the student's point of view, of what is going on in the sketch
4. *Slide show and podcast*, where the sketches are turned into photographs, and assembled into a slide show, which is later narrated with the scripts for a podcast
5. *Publication*, where the community publishes and distributes their narrated result in several media formats

The purpose of this work is for the school community to think through the implications of their transformation for the lives of their students, in very concrete terms. We are not at this stage hammering out a set of written statements that everyone can agree to; instead we are painting a picture of what our transformed school will look like through the eyes of a student. By the end of this step, the school community should have a clear and concrete idea of what their transformed schools will look like, agreement on the key elements of their transformation—the aspects of education that will be new and different, a clear idea of how the transformation will affect the day-to-day work of students and teachers; and a narrated slide show and podcast that can communicate their vision to the community.

The appendixes to this book contain samples and brief step-by-step instructions that may be useful at this step. As noted earlier, Appendix A contains sample Day in the Life stories from schools and districts that have been through this process. Appendix C contains step-by-step instructions for how to build the slide show and how to develop your slides into a podcast by adding narration, including how to rehearse and record narration.

Key Ideas and Illustrations

After recognizing the need for change and viewing the visions from other schools, the community needs time to discuss and digest the new ideas they have confronted. A good way to make this happen is to brainstorm the key ideas that you want to include in your own transformation and propose a concrete illustration of each.

The *key ideas* are the innovative principles that your transformed school is built on; the *illustrations* are vignettes that show a student manifesting that idea. A good vision will include about a dozen key ideas, with two illustrations for each one. After reviewing sample key ideas and illustrations from other schools (see Table 2.1 for a chart of key ideas and illustrations drawn up by a group of educators in New York), convene a working group to produce such a document for your own school.

You want to begin by generating as many ideas as possible. A good way to do this is to group participants into triads and ask each triad to produce three key ideas (with two illustrations each.) You may want to display their ideas on a projection screen or use Google Docs as an online brainstorming tool to gather these ideas quickly and enable the triads to see each other's work.

Educators tend at this point to describe very general goals with abstract illustrations that are not useful in building Education 3.0, such as,

TABLE 2.1. Sample of Key Ideas and Illustrations

Key Ideas[a]	Illustrative Examples[b]
Students work on small-group projects aimed at issues of community concern.	One group project focuses on the level of PCB's allowed by law in drinking water, and students work on the legal, environmental, and scientific aspects of this issue.
	Groups meet daily with their teacher and also at other times by themselves in specially designed spaces.
Academic work is coordinated with group projects and across disciplines.	A math lesson on statistical sampling coincides with the project group exercise in data sampling.
	Students read *Walden* in the English course as they study environmental issues in their project group and in the science course.
Students use a wide array of digital communication tools to accomplish their work.	Students conduct a WebEx video conference with a scientist at the EPA office in the state capital to learn more about measuring PCB levels in water.
	Students make extensive use of instant messaging to coordinate their group work throughout the day.
Students present their ideas to peers, teachers, and the community through digital multimedia publications.	Students report the results of their project study through a rich media podcast with graphs, video, tables, and animation.
	Students use Flip video cameras, iPod voice recording, and an array of still images to gather and illustrate their findings.
Students design a research experiment and collect real-time data with digital probes.	Students connect to the online municipal drinking-water measurement station to monitor the data in real time.
	Students connect various probes to their laptops in chemistry lab to measure levels of PCBs and other contaminants in water.

Note. [a] Concepts that distinguish your school from others and place it squarely in the 21st century. [b] Examples of what students do, in the classroom and elsewhere, to illustrate the implementation of each key

"100% of our students will be proficient in math" or "All our graduates will be career and college ready." Encourage them instead to be more concrete and specific, focusing on means as well as ends. Engage them in discussions that help them think through the implications of their ideas. Ask them, "What does it mean to be proficient in math? Give me a specific example of what a proficient student can do"; and later, "What exactly will students be doing to build that proficiency?" Refer again to Table 2.1 for the level of specificity that is needed at this step of the process.

Once the planning team has generated at least 20 ideas, let the group look at all of them and discuss them with their authors. Promote and encourage give-and-take here. Then review each illustration in turn, asking, "How well does this illustration communicate the essence of our vision?" Let the group put the ideas and illustrations in order based on this question, best illustrations first. The top 15 illustrations will go into sketches in the next activity.

Sketches

This is the key element of creating your vision of Education 3.0, where the planning team draws and talks through scenes in the Day in the Life of a student at their transformed school. The sketching is best done in groups of three to six, mixed by type. Ideally, each group includes at least one student, a teacher, an administrator, and a parent or citizen.

Each sketch should illustrate an instance in the Day in the Life of a student, through the student's eyes. The sketches will guide the production of the slide show that will communicate the vision to its various constituents. A good sketch should do several things:

- Illustrate what's happening from a student's perspective
- Include specific curriculum content with concrete examples
- Show what's in the student's hands
- Mention what's on the student's mind
- Refer to what's in the student's heart
- Show a scene that does not commonly happen today in the school
- Illustrate a key idea in this school's transformation

Each group should display and explain its sketch to the entire assembly, to allow a thorough discussion of each scene. Through these presentations and discussions the vision develops and solidifies in the minds of the participants. Most schools that have gone through this process do this sketching in several rounds, with a presentation and discussion at each round. Figures 2.1 and 2.2 show sample sketches.

FIGURE 2.1 . Sketch of a Group of Elementary Students in a Science Class

Scripts

The next task for the planning team is to write a script for each sketch (see Figures 2.1 and 2.2 for examples). The script should simply explain what's happening from the student's perspective. The script may be written from the first person perspective ("I enter the library with my iPad in my hand ready to meet with my project group...") or the third person ("Sally enters the library with her iPad in her hand ready to meet with her project group...") The simpler, more direct script works best. Authors should avoid educational jargon, buzzwords, or empty adjectives, and instead focus on the practical and concrete. Scripts should include answers to these questions:

- What's in their hands?
- What's on their minds?
- What's in their hearts?

Here is a sample script from a Day in the Life story for a high school:

FIGURE 2.2 . Sketch of an Elementary School Learning Center

I am an 11th-grade student. I begin my school day in the common room, where I connect to my personal online portal to check my schedule, chat with classmates, and review class notes. Students around me are doing many things: collaborating on a research project, video-chatting with their math tutor, and accessing textbooks on their portable devices.

Now I enter my Earth and Space Science class. Today we are studying the earth's divisions and their functions. In the front of the classroom a student leads a discussion, using Google Earth to describe the various components of the planet. At the same time, several study groups work at interactive computer tabletops, each interacting with a different part of the lesson. My group focuses on the location of populations. Group 2 looks at weather trends and their impact on people. Group 3 examines the polar ice cap and its effect on climate. Group 4 looks at natural disasters, weather, and climate. We all contribute to the discussion.

The whole lesson is being streamed live to other schools with whom we have been sharing resources. It's also being recorded for use by homebound or absent students. During all this, the teacher circulates, observes, monitors, facilitates discussion, and assesses what the students are learning.

From Scripts to Story

The sketches with their scripts begin to tell the story of Education 3.0 in your school. The next step is to develop the story into a compelling narrative.This is where you turn your collection of illustrations into a Day in the Life of a student. The task seems simple—just put the sketches into a sequence from dawn to dusk. But it's not that simple. Look back at Sally's day: Her assignments and activities were coordinated, and linked one to the next to tell a story. There's a beginning, a middle, and an end, with continuity and purpose along the way. This calls for some creativity.

Developing the Day in the Life story is like writing a screenplay. The basic plot needs to be fleshed out with actual examples, content, and action. Look at the *Day in the Life of A Student* at the beginning of this chapter, and at the stories in Appendix A, for ideas on how precise and creative they need to be.

It is not necessary to involve the entire group in coming up with the story line that sequences the scenes and links them together; in fact, an individual acting as editor has proven to be a more efficient means. No matter who does the work, make sure that the story line enables the best illustrations to take center stage.

Slide Show

The next task in setting the vision is to turn the story's sketches and scripts into a narrated slide show and podcast. Here are the steps in the production process:

- *Edit the script.* Study the scripts and sketches and figure out the best order for them. They might be ordered chronologically, beginning in the morning and ending at night; or by the ages of the students, from youngest to oldest; or in any other sequence that makes for a good story. Once ordered, copy and paste the scripts into a single document and edit for style. Rewrite as necessary to achieve a present-tense, practical, concrete, and consistent script that captures the spirit of the group's vision. To get an idea for style, read scripts from other schools, if possible. Send the draft script for review by key members of the visioning team before drafting the slides.
- *Draft the Slides.* Copy the script scene by scene into the presenter notes section, slide by slide, of PowerPoint or Keynote. Use an existing Day in the Life as a model. Then add images, slide by slide, to match the script. Build in images one after the

other to show action within each slide. You may use your existing sketches, photos that you develop with your own students,
or photos derived from other sources. Appendix D provides
step-by-step instructions for making a slide show. Most school
districts harbor at least one student or teacher familiar with this
kind of slide show production, so encourage them to perform
this work.

- *Review with the visioning team.* Send the slide show and script to
  the team for review and approval.
- *Produce slides and podcast.* Revise the slides as necessary. Then
  turn the slides into a podcast, and add a voice-over narration of
  the script. The narrator may be a member of the visioning team,
  or (better yet) a student from the school. (For instructions on
  how to produce a podcast, see Appendix D.) Also, export from
  the slide show a PDF file that contains the slides as well as the
  script. Both PowerPoint and Keynote can do this easily. Examples of Day in the Life slide shows and podcasts can be found on
  the Education 3.0 web site at ed3dot0.net.

Publication

Make available to the visioning team and other key contacts in the
school community the *Day in the Life* in four formats:

- The text of the script
- A slide show in PowerPoint or Keynote
- A PDF file of the slide show with notes
- A narrated podcast

Gradually circulate the *Day in the Life* among the visioning team and
the school community. This is best done by posting the files online where
they can easily be viewed and downloaded by all, perhaps on the school
or district's web site.

SELLING THE VISION

Now that the vision is published, in the form of a *Day in the Life*, it's
time to make sure all elements of the school community—especially the
governing board, parents, and other taxpayers—understand it and recognize its importance. Spread the vision as soon as possible, through whatever means are at your disposal:

- Send the podcast to the local television stations and ask them to play it.
- Put the podcast onto the school's web site.
- Ask the local newspaper to print the script of the narration.
- Ask the businessperson on the team to present the slide show at the next Rotary Club meeting.
- Ask the teacher on the visioning team to present the slide show at the next faculty or teacher's association meeting.
- Ask the school board member to present the slide show at the next school board meeting.
- Ask the administrator to present it at the next leadership meeting.
- Ask the student newspaper to print the script of the narration.
- Put the video of the presentation up on a kiosk in the school lobby.

Since the *Day in the Life* forms the basis of the next three steps, it's important that as many people as possible have seen and heard about it and talked about it.

If your *Day in the Life* is truly transformational, it will also be provocative. It will paint a picture of a school that's far different from the one you have. It will show a student engaged in work that many members of the school community never experienced themselves while they were in school. Many teachers will not be able to picture themselves working in such a school. Many students will wonder what's wrong with the school they enjoy today. Many parents will be concerned that this new school won't help their sons or daughters get into a good college or prepare for a good job.

Now is the time to engage this controversy. Don't wait until the vote on the bond issue—confront the issues now, at the visioning stage. Go back as necessary and help members of the school community recognize the need for change. Continue discussing the *Day in the Life* as you move forward with the next three steps in the process. If you've crafted it well, it will gather additional support the more it's subject to serious consideration.

CHAPTER 3

Scan the System

This chapter helps you determine the difference between your *Day in the Life* slide show and an actual day in the life of a student at your school today. It provides background and tools to help you to identify the gaps between your vision for the future and the reality of today. The chapter begins with a quick look at how your school today compares with your new vision, then delves deeper into what needs to be done behind the scenes to build Education 3.0. It suggests methods for you to use in understanding the important gaps. Along the way, it helps you analyze the two infrastructures—technical and educational—that exist in your school today and need to be modified to bring forth Education 3.0. It will consider all aspects of your operation: the manifestation of the principles of Education 3.0 in the lives of students; what's happening behind the scenes of Education 3.0, in respect to both the technical and educational infrastructures; and teachers' technology competence.

EDUCATION 3.0 INVENTORY

A good way to begin the process of scanning your system is to ask students and teachers and parents how well their current lives match the *Day in the Life* you just created. This kind of survey also serves to spread the vision among these important constituents of the school community and also helps them recognize the need for change.

Table 3.1 shows an example of what such an inventory might look like. The example was developed from the core principles and practical examples of the *Day in the Life of Sally* (see Chapter 2, "Principles of Education 3.0"); yours should grow out of your own vision, and so it won't be exactly the same.

Create your own version of this inventory and administer it to students, faculty, and students. Compile the results; they will help you see

TABLE 3.1. Education 3.0 Inventory

Education 3.0 Inventory

for _____ , taken on _____ .

How many of your students today...

Worked on Problems Worth Solving:	<25%	26-50%	51-75%	>75%%
...worked with a collaborative project group to solve an issue of public interest as well as academic importance.	☐	☐	☐	☐
...found the concepts in one subject fully coordinated with the topics and assignments of the others.	☐	☐	☐	☐
...learned the aspects of their subjects actually used in the real world, such as probability and statistics, estimation and measurement in math.	☐	☐	☐	☐
...worked at a community internship to build elements of character that complement academic work.	☐	☐	☐	☐

Collaborated Productively:				
...worked in a credit-bearing team project group with a faculty coach, during time allotted for this purpose within the school day.	☐	☐	☐	☐
...met with their peers in spaces designed especially to facilitate small-group project work.	☐	☐	☐	☐
...used desktop videoconferencing for distance-learning, discussions with subject-matter experts, guest speakers, or remote teachers.	☐	☐	☐	☐
...discussed with their families the ideas they encountered at school, using the family discussion questions from the school's web site.	☐	☐	☐	☐
...connected to multilingual, multicultural and international resources, and applied them to their academic projects.	☐	☐	☐	☐

Engaged in Self-Directed Research:				
... effectively searched online sources, determined their authority and reliability, and skimmed the search results to find what they seek.	☐	☐	☐	☐
... used real-time data from their own digital probes and from sources all over the world to explore issues and solve problems.	☐	☐	☐	☐
... used an extensive library of electronic texts, tutorials, and online courses that they downloaded to their laptops and iPods.	☐	☐	☐	☐
... used digital communication technologies to tap the knowledge of peers and online experts.	☐	☐	☐	☐
... completed much of their academic work – especially their independent and group project work – outside of school hours.	☐	☐	☐	☐

Learned How to Tell a Good Story:				
... employed images, video, music, and animation to bring deeper understanding to their academic work and presentations	☐	☐	☐	☐
... borrowed from the school's lending library of devices to make media capture and editing and display possible.	☐	☐	☐	☐
... published their work to an online multimedia portfolio that provides evidence of learning.	☐	☐	☐	☐
... presented the results of their work to an audience outside the school, combining oral presentation and digital media.	☐	☐	☐	☐

how much work you need to do to build Education 3.0. This inventory and other tools for scanning the system are available on the Education 3.0 website at ed3dot0.net.

This inventory measures the perceptions of your constituents, an important aspect of your understanding of what needs to be done. But it must be complemented by a serious examination of the underlying infra-

TABLE 3.1. Continued

Employed Tools Appropriate to the Task:

... used digital communication technologies such as instant messaging to work with teachers, peers, and community.	☐	☐	☐	☐
... listened to podcasts on mobile devices, that extended and enhanced their academic work.	☐	☐	☐	☐
... used digital tools such as videoconferencing, shared documents, and learning management systems to get their work done.	☐	☐	☐	☐
... used digital tools to develop animations, videos, presentations, and podcasts that supported their academic work.	☐	☐	☐	☐

Learned to be Curious and Creative:

... identified opportunities to extend their studies in new directions, then applied the necessary tools to get the job done	☐	☐	☐	☐
... were rewarded for discovering new patterns and relationships.	☐	☐	☐	☐
... applied artistic appreciation, composition, and expression to their problem-solving and academic work	☐	☐	☐	☐
... were assigned tasks that expected them to seek out new approaches and design unheard-of solutions.	☐	☐	☐	☐
... ended the day with a sense of wonder and curiosity linked to important academic objectives.	☐	☐	☐	☐

About your school

Number of students:

Number of faculty:

Grades or ages:

Start time and end time:

Graduation rate:

College entrance rate:

College completion rate:

structures that form the basis of these perceptions. So let's look behind the scenes of Education 3.0 and behind the scenes at your school.

BEHIND THE SCENES OF EDUCATION 3.0

The kinds of learning and teaching and leadership we see in the *Day in the Life* stories in this book—and in your own *Day in the Life*—would be impossible in most schools today. That's because they lack the infrastructure necessary to enable what Sally and Mr. Bacon (her science teacher) and Ms. Hunter (her superintendent) did during their busy days. Not just the technical infrastructure, but the teaching and learning infrastructure as well.

We can all imagine the cables and wires and routers and servers and computers and iPads that make up the technical infrastructure of the Education 3.0 school. Harder to picture is the teaching and learning infrastructure: the online content, the new teaching techniques, the varied schedule, and the cross-disciplinary planning that takes advantage of the technical infrastructure. Both types of infrastructure—technical and educational—are far different from what we see in most schools today. This chapter describes each type of infrastructure in some detail, beginning with the technical and moving to the educational.

TECHNICAL INFRASTRUCTURE

The work of the students and teachers pictured in the *Day in the Life* stories is supported silently and efficiently by an unseen set of technologies carefully planned and installed and maintained to support teaching and learning and leadership. This technical infrastructure consists of five elements:

- A robust network underlying the whole enterprise
- Reliable network services that provide what the people need to do their work
- An array of digital devices in their hands and backpacks and on their desks
- Powerful software that lets them create and communicate with these devices
- Solid curriculum content, in digital form, from respected authors, that helps students to learn and teachers to teach

Let's look at each of these elements in turn, so that we might be more informed as we scan our own system to assess their existence.

Robust Network

The network enables members of the school community to access the information and services they need from a variety of devices and places. The network provides entry to the school site from anywhere, so that students can study their academic materials whenever they need to. The local area network in an Education 3.0 school is tied directly to the Internet backbone with a fiber-optic connection, with wired backup, to ensure 24/7 reliability and the high bandwidth necessary for the kinds of work described in the *Day in the Life*. Within the school, wireless access points permit faculty and students to use a variety of devices wherever they are working. Outside of the school, a Virtual Public Network is used to provide members of the school community secure access identical to what they enjoy in the building.

> The network is like the foundation of a house: It supports everything else, but without the rest of the structure, it's not much to live in.

Reliable Network Services

Network servers provide the services that Education 3.0 students and faculty need to get their work done, from reliable and secure single-login, to mail and messaging, to more advanced and education-specific services, including the following:

- A learning management system that stores and presents course materials posted by teachers and projects created by students. It manages information about students and faculty: Who is enrolled in which course, when they are scheduled, what rights do they have to access information.
- An e-mail and messaging service that enables (and encourages) easy communication among members of the school community as well as with outside experts.
- Multimedia libraries containing educational audio and video collections used in teaching and learning, all fully indexed and available on demand.
- Attendance and parent communication systems that keep track of who is where and send messages to teachers and parents when they're not where they're supposed to be.
- Safety and security systems that monitor the building, entry points, and access to controlled areas.
- Video conferencing systems that permit communication by voice, video, graphics, text, and whiteboard.
- Online publishing services that let students, teachers, and school leaders communicate their own works safely and securely through the network, on web pages or through digital signage as appropriate.

The network servers and routers in an Education 3.0 school use open standards-based software and protocols for security, reliability, software choice, and ease of modification.

The network services are like the electrical and plumbing systems in a house: They require a firm foundation and are necessary to efficient modern living, but in and of themselves they are not sufficient to a happy household.

Digital Devices

The devices students and faculty use for learning and teaching in an Education 3.0 school range from large fixed equipment such as interactive projection screens, to desktop and laptop computers, to pocket-size iPods, iPad tablets, science probes, and small video cameras. The servers and network are specially designed to accommodate and encourage the use of such devices and to integrate them into academic work. Some belong to the school, but more and more belong to students and faculty personally. They are used for accessing information, communicating with others, and producing new works.

The digital devices are like the furniture and appliances in the house: resting on a solid floor, connected to the systems, and key to a useful life for the inhabitants.

Powerful Software

The software built into the digital devices that students, teachers, and leaders use at the Education 3.0 school enable them to read and watch and listen to most any type of media. But the real educational magic is when the users become creative producers: when they use these devices to tell their own stories, producing video clips, podcasts, slide shows, and multimedia reports, all of which can be shared and published through the network. This production software includes tools designed to:

- Capture and edit digital video and audio
- Collect, index, edit, and enhance images and photographs
- Assemble, create, and publish podcasts in audio, enhanced, and video formats
- Arrange effective slide presentations with images, text, diagrams, audio, and video
- Compose professional-quality print publications with flexible layout options
- Work with quantitative data and explore relationships with graphic representations

- Design and publish web pages and sites with full multimedia capability

All of these software tools are designed to work together, so that the output of one easily becomes the input of another, and vice versa.

> The software programs are like the utensils in the kitchen and the tools in the workshop that the inhabitants of the house use to accomplish their chores.

Solid Content

Neither the network nor the devices attached to it are of much use in the Education 3.0 school unless they can connect to solid content, published by respected authorities, and linked to relevant standards. Teachers and students produce some of their own content in this school, but not nearly all of it. The school licenses from major educational publishers the literature, history, science, languages, mathematics, and art references and tutorials their students need. These are selected by the faculty and carefully integrated into the projects and assignments of the students. This content runs through the network to be downloaded and displayed on the various digital devices in students' work areas and in their pockets.

> The curriculum content is like the food the family eats and the books they read and the subjects they discuss in the house: the items that nourish their minds and bodies.

Technical Infrastructure Analysis

Since this part of your system scan is based more on facts than perception, it might be best done as a survey among the leadership, including principals and technical staff. Develop a technical infrastructure table similar in form to the one below, but reflecting your own *Day in the Life*. Table 3.2 was based on *A Day in the Life of Sally,* and simply lists in the left column the elements of infrastructure necessary for Sally to do what she did. Yours may include different items. Distribute your analysis table as a survey to leadership and staff, compile the results, then convene a discussion to settle any areas of dispute. This technical analysis will show where the gaps lie and serve later to guide your development of a plan of action.

TABLE 3.2. Technical Infrastructure Analysis

Infrastructure Item *Robust Network*	We Have It Already	We Need It	How Important?	Comments
The network provides entry to the school site from anywhere, so that students can study their academic materials whenever they need to.				
The network provides the bandwidth necessary for the video and other tools used by students and teachers.				
Wireless access points permit faculty and students to use a variety of devices wherever they are working.				
A Virtual Public Network provides members of the school community secure access identical to what they enjoy in the building.				
Network servers and routers use open standards-based software and protocols for security, reliability, software choice, and ease of modification.				
Network Services				
A content management system stores and presents course materials posted by teachers and projects created by students.				
An e-mail and messaging service enables easy communication among members of the school community as well as outside experts.				
Digital multimedia libraries of audio and video items are used in teaching and learning, fully indexed and available through the network.				
Attendance systems keep track of who is where and send messages to teachers and parents when they're not where they're supposed to be.				
Safety and security systems monitor the building, entry points, and access to controlled areas.				

TABLE 3.2. Continued.

	We Have It Already	We Need It	How Important?	Comments
Video conferencing systems permit communication by voice, video, graphics, text, and whiteboard.				
Online publishing services let students, teachers, and school leaders communicate their works through the network as appropriate.				
Digital Learning Devices				
Students and faculty use interactive white boards, desktop IP telephones, laptop computers, iPods, science probes, and video cameras for teaching and learning.				
Servers and network accommodate and encourage the use of mobile learning devices.				
The software in the digital devices enables students to read and watch and listen to almost any type of media.				
Students use mobile devices to tell their own stories, producing video clips, podcasts, slide shows, and multimedia reports.				
Students share and publish these multimedia works through the network.				
Software enables students to capture, organize, and edit digital images, video, audio, podcasts, slide presentations, print publications, quantitative data, and web pages.				
Curriculum Content				
Online tutorials and references in literature, history, science, languages, mathematics, and art are available online to students.				
Curriculum content runs through the network to be downloaded and displayed on desktops and mobile devices.				

71

EDUCATIONAL INFRASTRUCTURE

It's not enough to simply buy and build the technical infrastructure described above. That, in fact, is the easy part of building Education 3.0.
The hard part is adjusting the methods of teaching and learning to take
advantage of the new technologies and to build the skills necessary for
the students' futures. Most of what surprises us in the *Day in the Life* stories of Sally and the others were not technologies, but radically altered
educational activities. These key alterations in the Education 3.0 school
include:

- What students learn
- How they learn it
- What teachers teach
- How they teach it

Let's examine each of these in turn. The path followed by Sally at H.S. 21+
scarcely resembles that taken by most high schoolers in America today.
Her steps covered different ground, and she ended up at a different place.
What Sally learned, and how she learned it, reflect a rethinking of the
purpose of school.

What Students Learn

The knowledge and skills that our students will need for their lives
and work in the future are different from those that we learned in our past.
While basic literacy and numeracy remain the price of entry to the new
workplace, they are not enough: The skills of collaboration, creativity, and
innovation are at least as important as mastery of the times tables. General problem-solving strategies are more important than the knowledge of
specific solutions. An understanding of the concepts of truth, beauty, and
justice is more important than knowing the difference between a gerund
and an ellipsis.

Thus Sally's assignments are grounded in reading, writing, mathematics, sciences, and arts; but they also require collaboration with other
students, provide extra rewards for creative analysis, and expect innovative solutions. The problems assigned by the teachers in most cases have
no single answer.

To design this new set of assignments was no easy task for the faculty
of H.S. 21+. They had to craft carefully into each assignment a combination
of solid content acquisition, along with collaborative problem-solving activities—and figure out how to evaluate the latter. Then they had to ensure

that all the assignments taken together formed a coherent package that comprehended the full set of competencies called for by the 21st century.

How Students Learn

During her day Sally spent much less time in a group of 25 in a classroom and much more time with a group of 5 or 6 in a library or laboratory. She spent less energy on paper-and-pencil tasks and much more energy on computer-based tasks. She seldom found herself performing the exact same task as the student next to her. She learned as much outside of the school building and day as she did inside.

Sally's day reflected the ways people work in the world outside of school. The learning methods at Sally's school stand in stark contrast to most high schools and require a heightened sense of self-discipline on the part of students, along with self-motivation and self-scheduling. Sally did not arrive at school with these traits—they were taught as part of the curriculum.

The methods of learning relied on technologies at every step—not "educational" technology, but real-world computer and network tools, the same ones used in the world of research and business, including technologies often banned in schools, such as instant messaging, video, and web publishing. All day long Sally applied common workplace technologies to serious academic tasks. This new form of learning calls for a different kind of planning and organization, a different set of expectations for students, and a new role for teachers, as well as the robust technology infrastructure described above.

Teachers

Few high school teachers today are asked to teach collaboration skills or problem-solving techniques, as Mr. Bacon did. Few are asked to coach a small group of students through a problem-solving exercise and then grade them on it. Few are required to coordinate their every assignment with their peers in other subjects. Teaching at an Education 3.0 school is nothing like teaching in a regular school. You must teach and evaluate not only the concepts of your subject area, but the new collaboration and innovation skills as well.

A teacher's work in Sally's school consists of two parts: standard subject matter teaching, and a project coaching assignment. Both types of work are carefully scheduled into the teacher's day. And the subject matter teaching is hardly standard—it's very carefully crafted to mesh in time with the problem-solving assignments and with the work of teachers in other subject areas. This scope of work calls for a wider range of skills on the part of the teacher: teaching techniques, curriculum planning expertise, and professional collaboration skills.

What Teachers Teach

The content taught at H.S. 21+ tends toward the applied and the practical. It focuses on those aspects of each subject that help students confront the group problem-solving tasks assigned to them. (For this reason, the problems must be carefully chosen so as to require a wide range of content knowledge for their solution.) Thus the decision of what to teach, and when to teach it, is much more in the hands of the faculty working as a whole.

How Teachers Teach

There's more *just-in-time* teaching at Sally's school, and less *just-in-case* teaching: just in time to apply it to the problem students are trying to solve in your group project; just in time to bring concepts from several disciplines to bear simultaneously on a common issue; just in time to provide a contrasting approach to what's being taught right now in another subject.

And teachers teach in different places, to different sizes of groups: in the auditorium to 150 students, in a classroom with 25, in a seminar space with 6. Teachers teach in different modes: a lecture here, a discussion there, a coaching session somewhere else. This calls for a richer repertoire of teaching skills than we are used to.

The reliance on technology that we saw in the *Day in the Life* stories —for finding information, for analyzing it, and for presenting one's findings—sets a high bar of expectations for the teacher, who must not only keep abreast of new technologies in his or her field, but find new ways to take advantage of them in the classroom.

Educational Infrastructure Analysis

This analysis is best performed by principals and a sample of teachers, using a similar process: Develop a table based on your own vision, distribute the table as a survey, compile the results, and convene a meeting to hammer out a consensus. Like the analysis of the technical needs of your vision, this analysis of the educational infrastructure (see Table 3.3) will outline what you need to include in your plan in Step 4 and what you need to build in Step 6.

TABLE 3.3. Educational Infrastructure Analysis

Infrastructure Item	We Have It Already	We Need It	How Important?	Comments
Assignments are grounded in reading, writing, and mathematics, arts, sciences, and humanities.				
Assignments require collaboration with other students, provide extra rewards for creative analysis, and expect innovative solutions.				
The full set of 21st-century skills are taught and assessed in the curriculum.				
Students spend spend less time in a group of 25 in a classroom, and more time with a group of five or six in a library or laboratory, or a group of 100 in a lecture hall.				
Students spend less time on paper and pencil tasks, and more time on computer-based tasks.				
Students seldom perform the exact same task as the student next to them.				
Students learn as much outside of the school building and day as they do inside.				
Learning relies on real-world computer and network tools, the same ones used in the world of research and business.				
All faculty are expected to teach collaboration skills and problem-solving techniques.				
Teachers coach a small group of students through a problem-solving exercise and then grade them on it.				
Teachers coordinate their every assignment with their peers in other subjects.				

At this point, having scanned the system to identify the educational gaps, most schools come to understand the important role that the skills of the teacher play in the process of building Education 3.0. So they want to look more closely at this aspect of their current status, and identify areas in which their teachers may not possess the skills necessary to their vision, especially those relating to the integration of technology into the days in the lives of their students.

TEACHERS' TECHNOLOGY COMPETENCE

How many of your teachers are prepared to lead their students through the *Day in the Life* that you have envisioned? This element of the scan of the system will help you toward an answer to that question. We'll begin with a discussion of the ways that teachers use technology in Education 3.0, then suggest a tool for surveying their competence in that regard.

Based on the work of schools moving toward Education 3.0 and of colleges preparing teachers to work in such schools, we have developed a list of the general and personal skills with computers, networks, and other devices that a teacher should be able to apply to the day-to-day tasks that are common to Education 3.0—and also common in Workplace 3.0.

The competencies in this list have been checked for validity against similar lists from the International Society for Technology in Education and state certification offices, and checked for reliability with the reports of more than 2,000 practicing teachers who participated in a teacher technology assessment during the past few years. The competencies are organized into five aspects: productivity, research, communication, media, and presentation. The sections below list the skills of a competent teacher in each of these areas.

Productivity

- *Produce and manage learning documents.* This includes composing standard educational publications such as parent newsletters and handouts for students and class lists; it also includes teaching students how to prepare their own documents on a computer so that they are readable and useful.
- *Analyze quantitative data.* This includes administrative work such as putting student test scores into a spreadsheet and analyzing them, as well as preparing curriculum materials with digital tables and graphs of curriculum content, and for some teachers

recording measurements from science experiments directly into the computer.

- *Organize information graphically.* The teacher can use specialized graphic organizer programs, as well as general tools such as word processors or presentation programs, to create digital representations of educational information, and includes these tasks regularly in assignments for students.

Research

- *Use effective online search strategies.* In their professional preparation, as well as in their classroom assignments, the teacher chooses the most appropriate research tools and databases and applies the most effective search techniques to produce useful and safe online resources in the classroom.
- *Evaluate and compare online information and sources.* Once located, the teacher knows the difference between authoritative and untrustworthy sources, how to ascertain authorship, and how to find sources with different points of view. He also can teach these skills to students.
- *Save and cite online information and sources.* The teacher knows a variety of methods for bookmarking and saving valuable online resources so that may easily be found later and employed in learning materials. She also can use accepted protocols for citing online sources and teaches these to students.

Communication

- *Communicate using digital tools.* These include e-mail, instant messaging, mobile phones, and text messaging for communicating with students, parents, and colleagues, and knowing how to organize and manage these tools in the classroom so that they can be used for learning.
- *Collaborate online for learning.* The teacher takes advantage of the tools listed above plus blogs, wikis, chats, and audio and video conferencing to bring outside resources into the classroom and to encourage academic collaboration among students.
- *Publish learning resources online.* From a simple web site to a complex curriculum wiki, to the online posting of student projects, to podcasting, the teacher has mastered an array of tools and techniques for publishing learning materials online.

Media

- *Differentiate instruction with digital media.* This includes an awareness of assistive technologies for disabled students as well as an ability to use a computer to prepare and present academic ideas in a variety of forms for better learning by all students.
- *Capture and edit images, audio, and video.* The teacher can use digital still and video cameras, edit their output on a computer, and produce learning materials that range from simple slide shows to the archiving of student presentations and performances.
- *Produce digital multimedia educational experiences.* The teacher can combine media from a wide array of sources into a useful presentation of academic content, and can teach this skill to students.

Presentation

- *Create effective digital presentations.* Using common tools for preparing slide shows, videos, and podcasts, the teacher can create presentations that follow the principles of communication and can apply these design principles to the evaluation of students' digital work.
- *Deliver digital multimedia presentations.* Using common devices such as computers, projectors, and screens, the teacher can set up classroom presentations, deliver them comfortably and effectively, and arrange for students to do the same.
- *Employ new media devices for learning.* From large SmartBoards to tiny iPods, to science probes, the teacher can incorporate a variety of digital devices into the instruction in the classroom and use them to extend learning opportunities for students outside of school.

Those are the skills that just about every teacher needs, no matter the subject or grade. Beyond these are the more specific technical skills required of a high school math teacher or a teacher of visually impaired students, competencies similarly necessary to build Education 3.0. The faculty of the School of Education at Hunter College in fact requires all teacher candidates to master these competenices; you can see their online system for ensuring competency at soe-server2.hunter.cuny.edu/assessment/.

To scan the readiness of your faculty to work with the key technologies of Education 3.0, administer a survey similar to what's shown below, but oriented to your own vision.

Faculty Technology Profile

This brief survey of 10 questions gathers information on how you are using technology in your teaching. The results will be used to help your school design a professional development program to build Education 3.0. The first section of the survey collects information on your teaching assignment and your technology. The next six sections cover the ways you use technology in your courses, in your teaching, for communication, with media, for productivity, and for research. The last section gathers your thoughts on professional development.

In each section, please read carefully all the responses, then choose the statement that best describes you.

1. About technology: Choose the phrase that best describes you.

☐ I use basic computer and network tools when it is necessary to get my work done. I accept my students' work from computer sources, but I neither encourage nor assign such work on a regular basis. Technology is not a central aspect of my teaching, but I'll use it if I must.

☐ I apply the basic technical tools—word processor, e-mail, and the Internet—to my research and teaching. Technology is here to stay, and may be important for my students to use. I'll use it in the classroom when it works, and when it's under my control.

☐ Technology allows students to employ multiple forms of expression in my classes, and I assign many projects that call for them to employ different media to help them learn a variety of topics. I want my students to have the opportunity to learn with today's tools; it's essential to their development.

☐ I look forward to learning new technologies as they appear and then quickly apply them to my teaching. Technology has enabled me to invent new ways of engaging my students with the content they need to learn.

☐ Technology has helped me transform the learning environment in my classroom. I experiment with new technologies as they appear. Technology is central to all that we do in class; it's the way we do our work.

2. In your courses: Choose the phrase that best describes you.

☐ I stick to tried and true approaches in my teaching, using standard textbooks, lecture, and discussion as appropriate. If my students use technology at all, it's on their own for research and writing their papers.

☐ I encourage students to employ the technology most appropriate to their work. I expect papers to be done on a word processor. I occasionally assign projects that require students to use digital technology.

☐ I often design new assignments that take advantage of the capabilities of the new technologies to develop key concepts. In fact, many of the activities in my classroom involve computers in one way or another, including a good deal of online learning.

☐ Most of my learning materials are posted online, and students use them to develop key concepts and higher level thinking skills. More and more of their assignments involve the application of digital tools to the solution of key problems, and most are submitted online.

☐ My courses direct students to employ cutting-edge technology tools to investigate concepts and solve problems. All relevant references and materials are posted online, and students often work on their assignments independently in collaborative groups.

3. In your teaching: Choose the phrase that best describes you.

☐ Most of the assignments in my courses involve written papers, as well as tests and quizzes done with paper and pencil. Use of the computer or the network by me or my students is incidental to the regular teaching in my courses.

☐ In my classroom, technology is used occasionally to deliver slide shows or display web pages, and my students are allowed (but not encouraged) to develop their assignments with digital media tools.

☐ My students often initiate projects that use technology, and many of my assignments expect them to employ computers in their work. Though multimedia projects are not easy to assess, I have developed criteria to judge the academic value of this kind of work, some of which my students create in cooperative group activity.

☐ I encourage my students to take the lead in finding new problems to solve and topics to explore, and bring them into class. They often locate useful online learning resources of which I was unaware. The results of their investigations become part of an online resource bank for my courses.

☐ Students in my courses initiate their own investigations into the course content, and use a variety of technical tools in this work. In large part they manage their own learning, and they design and publish their work as web sites and podcasts that are often consulted as learning resources by other students.

4. For communication: Choose the phrase that best describes you.

☐ I use e-mail when it's the only way to communicate, at home and for certain required tasks on campus. Most of my academic and personal communication employs the standard modes of telephone, face-to-face meetings, and written notes on paper.

☐ Many colleagues and students communicate with me by e-mail, and I encourage this. I've even tried instant messaging with a few of them. Some of my announcements to students and colleagues are published on the web for more efficient dissemination.

☐ Many of the assignments and materials for my classes are posted online. I have also found it valuable to use e-mail, IM, and other online forums and chats to share ideas with students, other faculty, and off-campus professionals.

☐ My web site has become a comprehensive resource bank for me and my students, with most assignments posted online. Students develop collaborative projects that are published on the web, and they often use instant messaging (including audio and video) to get this work done, among themselves and with me.

☐ Using instant messaging, video conferencing, podcasts, and blogging, my students extend their learning across the globe, and often collaborate across cultural and language barriers. They have begun to develop learning communities that are in constant touch with one another for the accomplishment of academic objectives.

5. With media: Choose the phrase that best describes you.

☐ If students include multimedia in their work, I accept it but do not expect such work as a matter of course. I use a digital camera at home for family photos, but seldom in my teaching. I know how to make a simple slide show on the computer, but I don't do so very often.

☐ Some of my course assignments require students to develop simple projects on the computer that include images. My own presentations to the class often include slide shows to illustrate key points.

☐ In my courses my students and I occasionally develop multimedia projects that explore key concepts. They have learned to use audio and video editing software, and can produce simple podcasts of their reports. The complexity of their digital storytelling is increasing.

☐ In my courses the students and I regularly produce original multimedia works in our field of study and publish these on the web, on DVD, and as enhanced podcasts.

☐ The multimedia projects produced in my courses are aimed at a broad audience and contain mostly original material developed from primary sources, in whatever media is most appropriate to communication and understanding.

6. For productivity: Choose the phrase that best describes you.

☐ Student writing assignments that are done on the computer are acceptable to me, and most of my composing is done with a word processor. I know how to save my files to the disk or flash drive and get the documents I need from the campus server.

☐ I prefer that students do their writing on a word processor, and I welcome their questions over e-mail. It's common for me and my students to use word processing, spreadsheets, and computer slide shows in their assignments. I know how to store these files on the campus server.

☐ In class we often analyze quantitative information with a spreadsheet or database to help us understand key concepts, and we also use computer tools specialized to our field. Students have learned to mark up each other's writing online using their word processors.

☐ In class or in the lab, we build simulations of natural and historical phenomena with spreadsheets and other digital tools. With these, students are able to design and carry out their own analyses of complex data. They frequently use the campus network for collaboration and for organizing their research materials.

☐ My students and I often devise new ways to use word processors, spreadsheets, and databases to explore the information in our field. I jump at the chance to learn a new software or hardware tool as soon as it appears and apply it to my teaching and research.

7. For research: Choose the phrase that best describes you.

☐ Most of the information in my courses comes from print sources, but I allow Internet research and sometimes use online sources for my lectures and discussions. I can find what I need on the Internet some of the time, but would rather work in the library.

☐ As a complement to their library research, students in my courses often find information on the web, usually through sources that I identify for them. Online research is an occasional part of the assignments in my courses.

☐ To help develop higher order thinking skills, I use online sources that send students to a wide range of information and ideas. Online research complements the books we used to use. I've begun to create an online archive of the most valuable sources in my field.

☐ My students are good at locating and evaluating new sources of academic information online and use these sources to raise issues and solve new problems. Internet research has pretty much replaced book research in my course, and the web has become the chief method for students to publish their own findings.

☐ The students and I publish our work in a variety of formats, including web sites, podcasts, and video documentaries. These works are often consulted by other students, scholars, and the community because of their educational value.

8. Please rate the **kinds of professional development** you need most, if you are to integrate technology into your teaching.

	Not at all	A little	Some	Quite a bit
Learning to use the new software tools that come with the computer				
Becoming aware of how technology applies to my subject area				
Developing presentations and assignments that employ technology in my courses				
Developing skills for using digital communication tools such as e-mail, instant messaging, and web publishing				
Learning how to post course materials online and receive student assignments electronically				
Developing skills for using digital media tools for incorporating images, sound, and video				

	Not at all	A little	Some	Quite a bit
Learning to use online research sources and tools				
Learning how to use word processing, spreadsheets, and other productivity tools in teaching				
Learning how to develop project-based learning assignments that employ new technologies				
Other				

9. Please rate the **styles of professional development** that would best meet your needs.

	Not at all	A little	Some	Quite a bit
Hands-on workshops on campus				
Teaching myself by trying out and learning new things on my own				
Learning informally from colleagues or campus technology specialists				
Learning informally from my students				
Online, self-paced courses that provide ideas and structured instruction				
Online courses with an expert who evaluates my progress				
Other				

10. Please rate the following **obstacles** to your integration of technology in teaching.

	Not an obstacle	A little	Some	Big obstacle
Lack of administrative encouragement and support				
Lack of effective professional development opportunities				
Lack of on-campus expertise and technical support				
Not enough computer access for my students				

	Not at all	A little	Some	Quite a bit
Computers that are inadequate to our educational tasks				
Lack of ideas for technology applications in my field				
Software that is not appropriate to our needs				
Slow or unreliable network connections				
Other obstacles				

TABLE 3.4. Instruments Used to Evaluate the Various Aspects of a School

Aspect	Instrument
Manifestation of the principles of Education 3.0 in the lives of students	Education 3.0 Inventory
Technical Infrastructure	Technical Infrastructure Analysis
Educational Infrastructure	Educational Infrastructure Analysis
Teachers' Technology Competence	Faculty Technology Profile

An online version of this Faculty Technology Profile is available on the Education 3.0 web site at ed3dot0.net

SYNTHESIZE THE SCANS

A complete scan of your system will compare your current status with your dreams for Education 3.0 and thus identify the gaps that you need to fill. And it will do this for all aspects of your operation, as shown in Table 3.4. Once the results of all of these have been compiled, the planning team should look them over and talk about them. This discussion will prepare your for the next step in the process.

CHAPTER 4

Plan for Action

The student in your *Day in the Life* carries out a multitude of educational tasks during the day. Each of these tasks calls for some sort of educational assignment and some sort of technology. To reach Education 3.0, you'll need to design these assignments and supply these technologies. This design and supply is your Plan of Action. This chapter shows how you can build the plan directly from your *Day in the Life* and your scan of the system.

You don't need a consultant or an engineer to develop your plan. You can do it yourself by studying closely your *Day in the Life,* considering what you learned from your system scan, and using a simple shared spreadsheet, such as Google Docs to record and keep track of the details.

DEVELOPING THE PLAN

The plan you will be developing is not a long document full of plati- tudes, beliefs, and rationales that goes into a loose-leaf binder on the shelf. Think of the plan instead as a detailed to-do list of what needs to be done to enable the *Day in the Life* to happen. We'll begin by looking at part of a sample plan drawn from Sally's school. Each item in the plan stems from an event in the Day in the Life story. For instance, in Sally's story,

> Sally wakes to the ping of an instant message arriving on her laptop. It's from another student at H.S. 21+ who is working with her on an environmental chemistry project.

So, to describe this more generally, the plan translates this event to a more genral description of what should happen, such as:

> Students and faculty IM each other with academic information in and out of school.

In order to enable this to take place, certain things need to be provided, including devices for students to use, a network that can manage instant messaging, and so forth. The plan describes these in turn:

> **Devices:** in the hands of students that can connect to the network from home and do instant messaging.
> **Network:** that can be accessed from home and manage instant messaging.
> **Curriculum:** that includes group projects that call for instant messaging among students.
> **Teachers:** who require and encourage collaboration between students.
> **Students:** who know how to use instant messaging for serious academic purposes.

The plan proceeds to the next event in Sally's *Day in the Life* story:

> She researches, from her laptop, the various laws and guidelines on allowable concentrations of PCBs in drinking water. She finds that the U.S. Environmental Protection Agency has set the Maximum Contaminant Level at 0.5 parts per billion.

This is translated to the generic:

> Students conduct online research.

And in order to enable this to happen, the plan describes what's needed, in the same categories:

> **Devices:** in the hands of students that can connect to the World Wide Web from home and conduct academic research.
> **Network:** that can be accessed from home and manage instant messaging.
> **Curriculum:** that includes group projects that call for instant messaging among students.
> **Teachers:** who require and encourage collaboration among students.
> **Students:** who know how to use instant messaging for serious academic purposes.

This third example starts from another event in Sally's day, and lays out the tasks necessary to enable it to take place:

On the subway on the way to school she listens to a podcast of last week's debate in the state senate on the Clean Water bill, that she downloaded from the school server.

Generalizing this to all students, the plan lists:

Students upload and download multimedia assignments and resources from home and school.

Then the plan looks into what needs to happen behind the scenes to make this kind of work possible:

Devices: in the hands of students that can connect to the school server from anywhere, and display multimedia learning materials.
Network: that can be accessed from outside the school and manage the distribution of learning materials.
Curriculum: with all materials available online in a variety of media formats.
Teachers: who prepare, post, and assign multimedia learning materials for use inside and outside of school.
Students: who know how to download and manage online multimedia materials for serious academic purposes.

The writing of the plan proceeds through every event in Sally's day, turning each into a generic goal, and then listing the tasks necessary to accomplish it. Table 4.1 shows an excerpt from a sample plan, drawn from Sally's story. A complete sample plan can be found in Appendix B. You will find on the Education 3.0 web site at ed3dot0.net a template for drawing up your own plan using this approach. To build your own plan, follow these six steps, one for each column on Table 4.1.

1. Describe a learning activity. Look at the first slide of your vision presentation. What is your student doing? What kind of learning activity is he engaged in? Let's say that in the first slide he is connecting to his online biology course from home just before breakfast, to download some illustrated readings to his iPod for study on his way to school. That's the learning activity. You'll put this in the first column of your planning table. To make the plan easier to understand, you'll describe the learning activity a bit more generically, such as: *Students download to mobile devices multimedia assignments and resources from home and school.* This learning activity will dictate the kinds of assignments and technologies you will need.

TABLE 4.1 Sample Plan of Action (excerpt)

Learning Activity	Devices . . .	Network . . .	Curriculum . . .	Teachers . . .	Students . . .
Students and faculty IM each other with academic information in and out of school.	in the hands of students that can connect to the network from home and do instant messaging.	that can be accessed from home and manage instant messaging.	that includes group projects that call for instant messaging among students.	who require and encourage collaboration between students.	who know how to use instant messaging for serious academic purposes.
Students conduct online research.	in the hands of students that can connect to the worldwide web from home and conduct academic research.	that can be accessed from home and support student research.	that includes assignments calling for extensive online research.	who prepare and post assignments calling for serious online research.	who know how to conduct effective online research for academic purposes.
Students upload and download multimedia assignments and resources from home and school.	in the hands of students that can connect to the school server from anywhere, and display multimedia learning materials.	that can be accessed from outside the school and manage the distribution of learning materials.	with all materials available online in a variety of media formats	who prepare, post, and assign multimedia learning materials for use inside and outside of school.	who know how to download and manage online multimedia materials for serious academic purposes.

2. Describe the devices in the student's hands. Start with what's in the student's hands, the hardware on which they'll download the assignment. Suppose your vision specifies an iPad, a popular mobile learning device. So, in the second column of the table, labeled Devices, you'll enter *Tablet-sized mobile device with Internet connectivity and multimedia capabilities.* It's important here to spell out exactly what the hardware needs to do, in this case be small enough to be carried and used on the school bus (*tablet-sized*), able to connect to the server where the assignment is stored (*Internet connectivity*), able to display the illustrated reading from an online course (*multimedia capabilities.*) If your description is not complete, you may not get what you need.

3. Describe the network services required for this learning activity. If the student could accomplish this task without connecting to the network, then you'd leave this column blank. But in the case at hand, the student needs a solid network connection from his device at home to the school's Learning Management System. And since most mobile devices use wireless connections, include this fact in your description: *Wireless web-based access to LMS system from home and school.*

4. Describe the curriculum development that neess to happen to enable the learning activity. Most Education 3.0 visions call for all learning materials to be available online, to be based on real-world problems, and to involve students in collaborative work. Enter in the next cell of your planning table the specific curriclum items that need to be developed to support the learning activity listed in the first column. *A problem-based curriculum with all materials available online in multimedia formats.*

5. Describe the skills teachers will need to make this learning activity happen. The downloading at home and study on the school bus will never occur unless teachers work this kind of assignment into the their courses. Most teachers have never taught with an online courses or mobile devices, so teacher development becomes a key requirement. Describe it here in the second-to-last column: *How to integrate a learning management system and mobile devices into the everyday curriculum.*

6. Describe the skills students will need to make this learning activity happen. We sometimes assume that our students already possess the technology skills they need to do the kind of learning activity we envision. Don't be so sure. List student development as a system requirement for each activity. In the current instance it might be: *How to access assignments from LMS, download them to a mobile device, and learn with them outside of school.*

What you have just done is to take a single vignette from your vision, and work it back through the network of devices, software, services, and skills that are necessary to make it happen. If your *Day in the Life* shows what's on stage, the plan shows what's behind the scenes. And as you can see, there's quite a bit of work to be done back there.

So continue on; take each and every vignette in your *Day in the Life*, describe it as a learning activity, and walk it back through to the various requirements. Not all learning activities will show an entry in each column, but most will involve several behind-the-scenes requirements. Don't be afraid to use the Sample Plan of Action, suggested at the book's website at www.ed3dot0.net—we compiled the sample from the work of more than 10 schools of all sorts.

Don't worry about repetition: You'll find that the same requirement shows up over and over, such as "laptop computer or mobile device with web capability," as being required for many different learning activities. The more times a requirement shows up in the table, the more important it is to your vision. Feel free to copy and paste as you complete the plan.

Once your planning table is complete, take it to your information technology department, or to your technology vendor, and ask them to start thinking about how they'd build the system that accomplishes all the functions listed in Columns 2–6. Take it also to your professional development staff and to your curriculum people, and ask them to look at the first and the last two columns and start thinking about how they'd make these educational changes happen.

SCHEDULE, RESPONSIBILITY, AND BUDGET

Each cell in your planning table needs to be accomplished for Education 3.0 to happen at your school. Therefore each cell needs a due date, a budget, and a person responsible to get it done. That's the very detailed work that will result in a complete plan of action. Think of it as the when, who, and how much for filling each of the gaps identified in your scan of the system.

Begin by creating a new table, and listing in the leftmost column all of the unique cells from your planning table. As we saw, many items are repeated over and over, since they are necessary elements of many of the educational activities. So even though "laptop computer or mobile device with web capability" appears repeatedly in the Sample Plan of Action (see Table 4.1) , you'll only list it once in the schedule spreadsheet.

Setting Due Dates

Some of the cells in the plan of action need to be accomplished earlier, since they are necessary to subsequent cells. For instance, a solid network infrastructure needs to be in place before digital devices are put in the hands of students, and teachers need to develop the outlines of the problem-solving curriculum before the instructional software can be selected. And some cells, such as teacher and curriculum development, will happen gradually over several years, and may in fact never be finished.

A good way to think this through is to create a new column in the spreadsheet, right next to the due date column, and label each item as follows:

1 = Needs to be accomplished early on, because it is necessary to the others.
2 = Is best scheduled after all the #1s have been done.
3 = Can wait until later in the implementation, perhaps in Year 2.
0 = Will be happening continuously, throughout the period of implementation and beyond.

You will find that many of the network infrastructure items will end up with 1s, digital devices and other equipment as 2s, and teacher and curriculum development as 0s. Certain advanced network capabilities, specialized devices, and architectural changes will get 3s. The numbering should reflect the relative importance of each item to your own goals, as well as the logical necessities mentioned earlier.

Once the general sequence numbers have been assigned, sort the spreadsheet by this new column and begin entering dates for each item: when we will start doing or installing it, and when it will be complete and ready for use. Month and year is sufficient detail at this point.

Assigning Responsibility

While the ultimate responsibility for all the events in the plan rests on the shoulder of the school or district leader, it's not wise to simply fill his or her name into every cell in this column. See the section on leadership in Chapter 6 for more detail on this issue. In fact, the more names that can appear in this column, the better; the further down the chain of command and deeper into the school community the responsibility extends, the better the end result. Let assistant principals, curriculum people, department chairs, teachers, and technical staff volunteer to take responsibility for the items that most interest them. They'll need a promise of leadership support and adequate budget to fulfill this responsibility effectively.

Determining the Budget

At this point in your planning you do not need bids and exact dollar amounts in the budget column. You are looking for an estimate of the cost of each row rounded to the nearest thousand. If you propose to purchase an iPad for every student, you need to multiply the number of students times what you'd expect an iPad to cost a year from now. If you need wireless access throughout the building, you might need to ask a vendor to provide you an estimate based on the architecture of your school and the number of devices to be connected. If you need to develop a dozen problem-based interdisciplinary curriculum units over the first summer, you need to estimate the number of teacher work days it will take multiplied by a fair daily rate.

Once you've entered an amount for each item in the list, you can sort it by date, and subtotal the amount needed in each year of implementation. As you read in the *Carson 3.0* example in the introduction , Education 3.0 takes more than a year to build out completely. And as the world changes, the conception needs to be refreshed and renewed.

In most schools the investment in the first year is the largest, since it includes about half of the technical infrastructure and a good start on the educational infrastructure. The second year allocates a larger proportion of resources to continuing teacher and curriculum development. In many schools, implementation is spread over several years, a grade-level at a time.

The schedule and budget spreadsheet forms the logistical outline of your plan. You can re-sort it to provide many different views of the work that needs to be done: by person, by date, by technical/educational dimensions, or by educational goal. But before you publish the plan in preparation for its adoption, think about how you will track and measure your progress toward Education 3.0. This assessment function needs to be built into the plan from the beginning.

An excerpt from a schedule drawn up by an Education 3.0 school is shown in Table 4.2, and a template for creating your own is included on the Education 3.0 web site at ed3dot0.net.

ASSESSMENT IN EDUCATION 3.0

- Did we accomplish our mission?
- Did it make any difference?

TABLE 4.2. Sample Planning Schedule

Item	July	August	September	October	November	December	January
Each student carries a digital device suitable for their work.	Write specs for digital device.	Get bids for devices.	Purchase devices.	Provide devices to teachers.	Provide devices to students.	Monitor use of devices.	Monitor use of devices.
Network							
The school provides a robust wireless network enables all devices to connect securely.	Write specs for network capacity. Conduct network analysis and tests.	Get bids for network improvements.	Install improved network. Test network.	New network in operation.	Monitor network operation.	Monitor network operation.	Monitor network operation.
The school provides network services and software to enable messaging and the management of learning materials.	Write specs for network software.	Get bids for network software.	Install network software. Test operation.	Network software in operation.	Monitor network software	Monitor network software	Monitor network software

94

TABLE 4.2. Continued

Curriculum

Learning materials are all available in digital form.	Set standards for digital learning materials.	Develop digital learning materials.	Develop digital learning materials.	Develop digital learning materials.	Post digital learning materials to LMS.	Post digital learning materials to LMS.	Post digital learning materials to LMS.
Interdisciplinary project assignments developed and posted, that focus on real-world social and technical issues worth solving.	Set standards for interdisciplinary projects.	Develop interdisciplinary projects.	Develop interdisciplinary projects.	Develop interdisciplinary projects.	Post interdisciplinary projects to LMS.	Post interdisciplinary projects to LMS.	Post interdisciplinary projects to LMS.

Teachers

Teachers know how to develop digital learning materials.	Show teachers how to develop digital learning materials.	Coach teachers as they develop digital learning materials.	Coach teachers as they develop digital learning materials.	Coach teachers as they develop digital learning materials.	Show teachers how to post digital learning materials to the LMS.	Teachers post digital materials to the LMS.	Teachers post digital materials to the LMS.
Teachers know how to develop project-based assignments with embedded academic skills, that focus on real-world social and technical issues worth solving.	Teachers help set standards for interdisciplinary projects.	Teachers learn how to develop project-based assignments.	Teachers develop project-based assignments.	Teachers develop project-based assignments.	Teachers post project-based assignments to LMS.	Teachers post project-based assignments to LMS.	Teachers post project-based assignments to LMS.

- How did our work change the lives and learning of students?

You need to build into your plan some mechanisms for answering these questions down the road. This section of the chapter provides some advice on how best to measure the effects of the changes you made for Education 3.0.

Start thinking about your assessment plan by perusing the *Day in the Life* you developed in Chapter 2 . Implicit in that story are some very measurable goals, and it is these that you should assess. Here is a list of goals from a school that went through the Education 3.0 process:

- We'll be able to do things not currently possible, such as collaborative writing among students.
- Our students will be able to access digital tools any time, any place.
- Students will learn to manage their time better.
- The materials and methods for learning will be richer.
- Students will be powerful creators of multimedia.
- We'll change our pedagogy and use more online resources.
- We'll see deeper learning and more inquiry-teaching.
- Our school will be more marketable.
- We'll use less paper.
- We'll agree on consistent content.
- We'll see more teacher collaboration.
- Students will be more motivated.
- Parents will help students learn.
- Students will show enthusiasm for writing, and for school.
- We'll see solid engagement in learning.
- Students will share with peers what they learn.
- Students will understand ethical issues with technologies.
- We'll see more efficient learning.
- We'll have more time for new things.
- We'll move from didactic to dynamic learning.
- Students will serve as teachers and leaders of learning.
- Students will work in groups, speaking, and engaged .
- We'll make multimedia links with Australian schools.
- They had high expectations for what Education 3.0 would do for their school. How would they assess whether or not they met their expectations?

Looking closely at the goals in the list above, we can see that each one is assessable—we can set up a way to measure how well we have accomplished each one. Not with a single instrument or test or survey of course, but through a variety of measures that can be repeated over time. Consider including many components in your assessment. Assess how students have changed, how faculty have changed, and how the perceptions of parents and community have changed. For each audience, design an array of assessment tools to measure the change. If you have followed the seven-step process along the way, you will find that you have already developed much of what you need to conduct this comprehensive assessment plan.

Assessing Change in Students

To assess how students have changed, and whether they are living the days in the life set forth in the vision, you may use a variety of measures:

- Measure what kinds of activities students are engaged in by using an observational walk-through, conducted by an administrator, quantifying the specific items listed in the vision. You may find that the Education 3.0 Inventory (see Table 3.1) that you developed in Step 3, Scan the System, makes a perfectly capable observational walk-through instrument.
- Measure the perception of students and how it changes over time by conducting a student survey at regular intervals. The items on the student survey can be drawn from the vision; you want to ask students how close the school is to implementing its vision. For this purpose, your Education 3.0 Inventory can be used as an annual student survey to assess how students see the progress of reform.
- Measure also other factors associated with student satisfaction with school, such as attendance and graduation rates, that you expect to increase as the school implements its vision. Let the year-to-year change in these numbers form a part of your assessment.
- Assess student achievement, the kind that is measured by standardized tests, as well as other kinds of learning mentioned in the vision. While you cannot expect to see an increase in state-administered standardized test scores as a result of your work since these tests measure for the most part the skills of Education 2.0, consider adding other standardized tests designed to measure the skills of Workplace 3.0 to the mix of the assessment plan.

TABLE 4.3. Assessments for Measuring Change

Goal	Instruments	Frequency
Student engagement	Education 3.0 Inventory, attendance rate, graduation rate	Annual
Faculty engagement	Faculty Survey (based on Education 3.0 Inventory), Faculty Technology Profile	Annual
Education 3.0 methods	Education 3.0 Inventory, Education 3.0 walk-throughs	Annual
Mastery of academic content	State mastery test, student portfolio	Annual
Mastery of Education 3.0 skills	Student portfolio, day-to-day assessments, Critical Thinking Test	Annual

Assessing Change in Faculty

To assess how the faculty is changing, administer the faculty technology profile annually, assessing how technology is incorporated in each teacher's work. Also administer a faculty survey, based on your Education 3.0 Inventory (see Table 3.1), to assess the faculty's view of how the vision is progressing. And consider capturing video of teaching and learning in the classroom, and then analyzing it to measure the kinds of new schoolwork called for in your *Day in the Life.*

Assessing Change in Parents' Perceptions

Ask parents to report their perceptions of how close the school is to achieving its vision. A reworded Education 3.0 Inventory (Table 3.1) can be used for this purpose.

Your assessment plan will include several items, similar to what is shown in Table 4.3.

Results of Assessments

All of these assessments, except the change in parents' perceptions, were conducted when you scanned the system; those results can be used as a baseline for comparison with annual repetitions of the same surveys and data collection. Some assessment results change quickly as the program is implemented; other things hardly move at all. In schools that en-

FIGURE 4.1 Trends of Various Types of Assessments

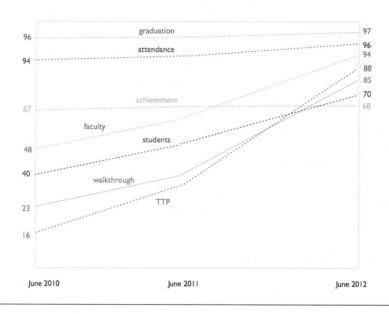

joyed high attendance rates, graduation rates, and achievement test scores when they started, we don't see a big shift—they were close to the ceiling at the outset, and so Education 3.0 cannot be expected to move these measures much farther up. The assessments that show the biggest change are those that measure student and faculty behavior and perception.

More than likely, you'll find something like the trends shown in Figure 4.1.

Some schools moving toward Education 3.0 look for a quick and easy assessment instrument that will result in a single number that represents how well they are doing at meeting their goals. Before following them along this road, consider the ideas in the next section.

A Grain of Salt

Examine the list of goals you have established for the students in your Education 3.0 school. If you are like most, your list will resemble the one published by the Partnership for 21st-Century Skills (http://www.p21.org/overview), a consortium of schools, businesses, and education groups that includes Apple, Cisco, Ford, NEA, Pearson, and ASCD, among many others. Here is what they say is important for every student to learn:

Mastery of Core Subjects

- English language arts
- World languages
- Arts
- Mathematics
- Economics
- Science
- Geography
- History
- Government and civics

Mastery of 21st-Century Themes

- Global awareness
- Financial, economic, business, and entrepreneurial literacy
- Civicliteracy
- Health literacy

Creativity and Innovation

- Think creatively
- Work creatively with others
- Implement innovations

Critical Thinking and Problem Solving

- Reason effectively
- Use systems thinking
- Make judgments and decisions
- Solve problems

Communication and Collaboration

- Communicate clearly
- Collaborate with others

Information, Media, and Technology Skills

- Access and evaluate information
- Use and manage information
- Analyze media
- Create media products
- Apply technology effectively

Life and Career Skills

- Adapt to change
- Be flexible
- Manage goals and time
- Work independently
- Be self-directed learners
- Interact effectively with others
- Work effectively in diverse teams
- Manage projects
- Produce results
- Guide and lead others
- Be responsible to others

These are the skills that Sally's school and many others are striving to develop. Could any single test ever hope to come close to measuring all of these skills? An analysis of the mastery test required by a major northeastern state found that 90% of the questions focused on only 2 of the 38 skills in the list above: mathematics and English language arts. The remaining 10% measured critical thinking and problem solving. But none of the questions measured the other 34 skills.

We have developed a lucrative industry around measuring a small subset of math and reading skills—those that are easy to measure with multiple-choice tests, but not all that critical to future success. And we spend inordinate amounts of time and money teaching and testing them. But they account for less than 5% of the things students ought to learn in the Education 3.0 school.

If we wanted to evaluate a restaurant, we would send a sensitive gourmet to eat a full meal and write up the entire experience; if we wanted to be more thorough, we would send a second critic with different tastes. The critics would describe the atmosphere, the smells; the presentation of the food, its taste, texture, and color; the service; the harmonization of the wines; the quality of the silverware, napkins, salt, and pepper. Readers would have a comprehensive sense of the quality of the place.

If we applied Education 2.0 educational assessment logic to this problem, we wouldn't do it that way. Instead, we'd look for a subset of the whole that's easy and quick to measure, such as the quality of the salt. We'd develop a rubric to describe the various degrees of salt quality, and perhaps even develop a special magnifying glass so we can see the individual grains, and a picture card to match the grains to a 5-point standard scale. We'd send a minimum-wage inspector out to the restaurant and get results for dozens of them each day. Very inexpensive, yet producing reliable, accurate results, that no one could argue with. Significant to the .05 level if you desire.

My grandmother used to tell me concerning my grandfather, who was wont to exaggerate, "Take everything he says with a grain of salt." When I was very young, I wondered what she meant—should I grab the salt shaker whenever he started telling one of his stories? It took me a while, but I figured out her figure of speech. (My grandmother didn't know it, but this phrase has its origins in the Latin *cum grano salis*, a way to make insipid food go down easier.)

AN EDUCATION 3.0 FEAST

There's more to this meal than meets the eye. If we allow a few grains of salt to determine the quality, we'll soon be disappointed in our eating. Restaurants will learn to game the system, focusing on the condiments at the expense of the main dish—getting good reviews but serving mediocre food.

So stop looking only at the salt, and consider the entire panoply of skills as we assess your students and your schools. Pay more attention to the other 34 essential skills that aren't on the state mastery tests. And teach them seriously. Hold yourself accountable for your students learning them. We won't move from Education 2.0 to 3.0 by pondering the salt. And the next time someone touts their "high-performing school," based on their state mastery test scores, take their claim with a grain of salt.

If you want to move beyond the salt in your assessment plan, how would you do it? This section of the chapter proposes a plan for assessing student progress in Education 3.0, and employing digital technology fully in the process.

Though many schools today claim to develop the wide range of skills and ideas students will need in Workplace 3.0, few assess them with any regularity. Instead, they administer the tests developed to measure Education 2.0: the state mastery test, the CTBS (Comprehensive Test of Basic skills) or the ITBS (Iowa Tests of Basic Skills), the PSAT and SAT, and the Regents tests. And they measure their success by the scores from these Education 2.0 tests. And as we learned, these assessments measure but a small subset of what students needed to know in the mid-20th century, and little or nothing of what they need to know for today—or tomorrow.

Don't fall into the salt mine as you prepare your assessment plan. Don't look for a single, 15-minute test that gives you a nice, neat score on everything that's important. Many vendors would like to sell this to you. Don't bite. One such company touts an online test of modern technology skills, complete with quartiles, statistics, and graphic districtwide reports. Let's look more closely at how it works. One of the questions is *Which of these is a picture of a computer?*, Followed by drawings of an igloo, a cow, an apple core, and a computer. This is probably not what you had in mind when you considered Education 3.0.

But without such a standardized test, how will we know if are students are learning the new skills? How will we know if we're doing better than last year, or better than our neighbors? Consider a three-prong approach to assessment:

- Day-to-day assessment in the classroom
- Structured online portfolio for every student
- Comparable standard tests

Day-to-Day Assessment in the Classroom

As you design the professional development aspects of your plan, prepare every teacher in every classroom to teach Education 3.0 skills and content and also to assess them. Include time for teachers to include such assessments in their required assignments. Show them how to award grades based on the performance of Education 3.0 skills, so that a B+ in English represents not only knowledge of Shakespeare but ability to collaborate with a diverse group of peers.

Let the faculty determine when and where and how the Education 3.0 skills and concepts will be taught and assessed. Faculty should, for each course or problem-based learning project, make a list of which of the skills from your list will be included, getting right down to the specific assignment in the syllabus. Consider the following example listing some of the skills for English 10 with the specific assignment given next to each skill:

Think Creatively: Poetry composition assignment
Work Creatively with Others: Drama production task
Make Judgments and Decisions: Moral dilemma discussion
Communicate Clearly: Oral presentation assignment

This will uncover the skills that need more attention; the faculty will need time allotted in your plan to develop new assignments and assessments to ensure that all the skills are included across the curriculum. The important thing is that the Education 3.0 skills are assessed every day, and that they count in a student's grade.

Creating these day-to-day assignments with assessments will increase the probability that all students learn some of the new skills, and that some learn all of them—and that everyone pays more attention to them. But it's not a guarantee. A student could get a passing grade in all of his courses, and yet not be fully ready for the 21st century. We need something more to ensure that every student can demonstrate all the skills.

Structured Online Portfolio

Many of the Education 3.0 skills and content cannot be measured by paper-and-pencil assignments or multiple-choice tests, for example, the ability to work collaboratively with a diverse group or to illustrate the nature of self-reliance in *Robinson Crusoe*. These kinds of skills are best assessed though video clips or multimedia projects submitted by students and evaluated by standard rubrics. How do we implement something like this?

1. Prepare your list of skills.
2. Choose those that are best evaluated through the portfolio method.
3. Publish a rubric for each one that details what is expected for mastery.
4. Require that every student submit a digital document online—a video clip, a multimedia report, or a statistical analysis, for instance—that proves his or her mastery of the skill.
5. Assign faculty members to evaluate the submissions anonymously and online.
6. Make completion of the portfolio a graduation requirement for every student.

Because the students' work products are clearly defined and judged by teachers who did not have them in class, they become more independent measures of performance than classroom-based assessments. And because they include multimedia documentation, such as video clips of students at work, they can more accurately measure the social aspects of many of the skills. Research has found that concrete rubrics can make these kinds of assessments just as statistically reliable and valid as the bubble tests we are all used to.

Not everything goes into the portfolio; only those items that are best assessed through documentary evidence. And the completion of a useful portfolio—one that's aimed at a public audience—can serve as a motivating force for students as they move through their school careers.

Comparable Standard Tests

As a complement to the day-to-day assignments and the structured portfolio, consider administering a summative, standardized test that includes some of the Education 3.0 skills. This can provide information that the classroom-based and portfolio systems cannot: information to compare your school with others, and to compare your school's performance year to year.

The available tests in this genre do not cover all the skills in your list; they sample just a few. And their limited testing formats do not enable a full assessment of some of the social and performance-based aspects of the skills. But as a complement to the others, these tests can be very useful. The good tests are not inexpensive, because they go far beyond the simplistic multiple-choice style in the example mentioned earlier. I discuss four possible tests here.

College and Work and Readiness Assessment (CWRA). This test was designed by The Council for Aid to Education, a national nonprofit organization established in 1952 to advance corporate support of education and to conduct policy research on higher education. It measures how students perform on constructed response tasks that require an integrated set of critical thinking, analytic reasoning, problem solving, and written communication skills. The CWRA is delivered entirely online in a setting proctored by your own faculty. It costs $40 per student (at the time this book was written), and includs a complete set of statistical reports. Here's a sample of an item from the CWRA:

Introductory material: You advise Pat Williams, the president of DynaTech, a company that makes precision electronic instruments and navigational equipment. Sally Evans, a member of DynaTech's sales force, recommended that DynaTech buy a small private plane (a SwiftAir 235) that she and other members of the sales force could use to visit customers. Pat was about to approve the purchase when there was an accident involving a SwiftAir 235. Your document library contains the following materials: [the test manual contains the actual documents listed below]
1.   Newspaper article about the accident
2.   Federal Accident Report on in-flight breakups in single-engine planes
3.   Internal Correspondence (Pat's e-mail to you & Sally's e-mail to Pat)
4.   Charts relating to SwiftAir's performance characteristics
5.   Excerpt from magazine article comparing SwiftAir 235 to similar planes
6.   Pictures and descriptions of SwiftAir Models 80 and 235

Questions:
1.   Do the available data tend to support or refute the claim that the type of wing on the SwiftAir 235 leads to more in-flight breakups?

2. What is the basis for your conclusion?
3. What other factors might have contributed to the accident and should be taken into account?
4. What is your preliminary recommendation about whether or not DynaTech should buy the plane and what is the basis for this recommendation?

Which of our 21st-century skills is this measuring? How does the situation in the sample question compare with what happens in the world outside of school? Enough schools are using the CWRA that national comparisons are possible, and change over time can be measured.

The California Critical Thinking Skills Test (CCTST). This is a multiple-choice test widely used in business to measure thinking skills, one of the elements on everyone's list of Education 3.0 skills. It was developed by qualified psychometricians and has been used for many years. Here's a sample question:

Using the phone at her desk, Sylvia in Corporate Sales consistently generates a very steady $1500 per hour in gross revenue for her firm. After all of her firm's costs have been subtracted, Sylvia's sales amount to $100 in bottom line (net) profits every 15 minutes. At 10:00 a.m. one day the desk phone Sylvia uses to make her sales calls breaks. Without the phone Sylvia cannot make any sales. Assume that Sylvia's regular schedule is to begin making sales calls at 8:00 a.m. Assume she works the phone for 4 hours, takes a 1 hour lunch exactly at noon, and then returns promptly to her desk for 4 more hours of afternoon sales. Sylvia loves her work and the broken phone is keeping her from it. If necessary she will try to repair the phone herself. Which of the following options would be in the best interest of Sylvia's firm to remedy the broken phone problem?

A = Use Ed's Phone Repair Shop down the street. Ed can replace Sylvia's phone by 10:30 a.m. Ed will charge the firm $500.
B = Assign Sylvia to a different project until her phone can be replaced with one from the firm's current inventory. Replacing the phone is handled by the night shift.
C = Authorize Sylvia to buy a new phone during her lunch hour for $75 knowing she can plug it in and have it working within a few minutes after she gets back to her desk at 1:00 p.m.
D = Ask Sylvia to try to repair her phone herself. She will probably complete the repair by 2:00 p.m.; or maybe later.

As you can see, the format reminds you of the bubble-tests described above. But the content is quite different. The focus is on a subset of thinking skills, an area often included in Education 3.0 lists, but not often measured by the tests most of us use today. The CCTST is certainly not a comprehensive measure of what we are looking for, but it could serve as a statistically comparable sample.

Programme for International Student Assessment (PISA). This assessment has since 2000 been gathering information on the relative performance of 15-year-olds in more than 60 countries. It's run by the Organization for Economic Cooperation and Development, a respected intergovernmental agency. The skills and content they focus on, though not inclusive of all the Education 3.0 skills, certainly come closer than most of the tests in common use today. And their methodology seems to be closer to what we are looking for. Here's a sample question:

Mathematics Unit 44 : Decreasing CO_2 levels. Many scientists fear that the increasing level of CO_2 gas in our atmosphere is causing climate change. The diagram below shows the CO_2 emission levels in 1990 (the light bars) for several countries (or regions), the emission levels in 1998 (the dark bars), and the percentage change in emission levels between 1990 and 1998 (the arrows with percentages).

Question 44.1. In the diagram you can read that in the USA, the increase in CO_2 emission level from 1990 to 1998 was 11%. Show the calculation to demonstrate how the 11% is obtained.

Question 44.2. Mandy analyzed the diagram and claimed she discovered a mistake in the percentage change in emission levels: "The percentage decrease in Germany (16%) is bigger than the percentage decrease in the whole European Union (EU total, 4%). This is not possible, since Germany is part of the EU." Do you agree with Mandy when she says this is not possible? Give an explanation to support your answer.

Question 44.3. Mandy and Niels discussed which country (or region) had the largest increase of CO_2 emissions. Each came up with a different conclusion based on the diagram. Give two possible 'correct' answers to this question, and explain how you can obtain each of these answers.

FIGURE 4.2. CO$_2$ Levels, as Illustrated for Mathematics Unit 44

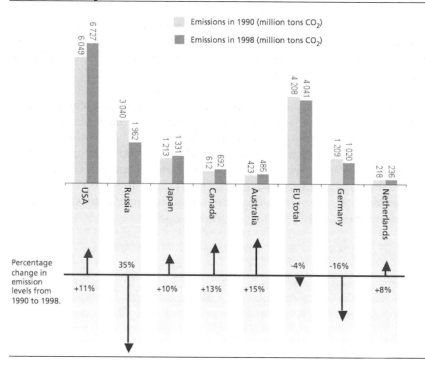

Makes you think, doesn't it? The content of the question relates to one of the themes from the Partnership for 21st-Century Learning (see list above in section called "A Grain of Salt"), as well as several of the math and science topics from Core Knowledge. And the skills and understanding necessary to complete the question draw from at least three from the same lists.

Unfortunately, PISA is not available for purchase by schools. It uses a sophisticated sampling procedure, so that not every student takes every test; and the scoring of the open-ended questions requires time and training that most of us are not willing to invest in. But a school that wanted to compare itself, over time and across countries, could administer the PISA questions, samples of which are available online (at http://www.pisa. oecd.org/dataoecd/47/23/41943106.pdf), do its own scoring, and gather some very useful information.

Triangulation

When you're sailing along the coast, you need the bearings to at least three landmarks to determine where you are. Even with a modern GPS, you need the information from at least three satellites to figure out your position. So when you want to assess Education 3.0, it may be best to assess from three points of view: in the classroom, day to day; through structured student portfolios; and with relevant standardized instruments. The combination of information from all three may help you know where you are, and guide you toward your destination. For further reading, consider 21st-Century Skills Assessment, from the Partnership for 21st Century Skills (see http://www.21stcenturyskills.org/documents/21st_century_skills_assessment.pdf), and FAQ on Assessment from Core Knowledge Foundation (see http://coreknowledge.org/CK/about/FAQ/FAQ_testing.htm).

CHAPTER 5

Adopt the Plan

Your vision and plan is developed, and at this step needs to be adopted by the proper authorities. In most jurisdictions you will find many people who believe themselves to have some authority over what their schools look like: the governing board, whether private or public; the teachers, whether unionized or otherwise; the parents who send their children to the school; the mayor or city council or governor of the municipality; and the students whom the school is designed to serve. The most successful plan for Education 3.0 will be adopted by all of these groups, in one way or another: Some will take formal votes, some will conduct consensus-building discussions, some will take it to heart. In this chapter we look at the who, what, why, when, where, and how of getting the vision and plan adopted.

WHO

The governing board that sets policy and the board that provides funds for the school are the most important adoptees. Without their support, Education 3.0 cannot happen. So your work in Step 5 needs to focus on their adoption. But governing board members are in most cases influenced by the views of their constituents: parents, students, voters, taxpayers, businesspeople, and teachers. A wise adoption strategy works on all these groups simultaneously, making sure that you've built support among the influencers before you propose the plan to a formal vote by the governing board. If you involved these varied constituents in the visioning process from Step 1, your chances for a successful adoption increase.

WHAT

Don't make the mistake of asking the budget authority to allocate funds for your Education 3.0 work without first understanding the vision and the plan. What's being adopted at this step is the entire package: vision, plan, and budget. The budget makes little sense without the plan, and the plan makes little sense without the vision. Keep all three together and you'll experience more success.

WHY

This is the first question people will ask you about the plan: Why are we doing this? What's wrong with the schools we have? So your adoption package must deal with this question at the outset. Review Chapter 1, "Recognize the Need for Change," to help you answer this question for your constituents. If you did a good job at the visioning stage, and circulated the vision and its rationale throughout the school community, then the why question will be easier to answer here in Step 5.

WHEN

In most jurisdictions there is a cycle of adoption and budgeting of school matters: an annual report, accompanied by a budget request, that takes place in the spring or fall of each year. There's a similar cycle for adopting new policy, that includes introduction to the board, study by a committee, hearings, and finally a vote to adopt. The timing of the adoption of your plan needs to take into account both of these cycles. Most schools moving toward Education 3.0 start the policy adoption process early on, as soon as they have developed their vision, presenting it for study well in advance of the detailed plan and budget request. After appropriate study, the governing board votes to move its schools toward the vision of Education 3.0 as manifest in the *Day in the Life;* later on, the presentation of the detailed plan of action and budget will come as no surprise.

WHERE

Adoption of your plan for Education 3.0 will not happen one night in a boardroom with a quick vote. Adoption evolved much earlier, perhaps over the course of a year, as you discussed the need for change with the PTA in the cafeteria in Step 1; then again when your presented your *Day in the Life* at the Rotary Club in Step 2; again as students at their desks reflected on the questions in the Education 3.0 Inventory in Step 3; and as principals in their offices assigned themselves responsibility for certain elements of the plan in Step 4. An effective process of change involves activity in many venues.

HOW

Just as members of your visioning team took the *Day in the Life* presentation out to their colleagues to get feedback and build support, these same team members may now be asked to take the entire package—vision, plan, and budget—out to their groups and gather momentum for its adoption. Make this easy by providing the vision and plan in several published forms: a printed brochure, a more detailed booklet, a podcast, a web site, all available online as well as in traditional forms. You'll need a 1-page, a 5-page, and a 30-page version of the printed material, each in more detail; the same for the podcast and web page: some will want a 5-minute explanation, others will need 30 minutes. Many more people will read and listen to the shorter versions than the longest and most detailed. Use these to gather support long before the scheduled votes to adopt and to fund.

CHAPTER 6

Build Education 3.0

Building Education 3.0 in your school can be a life's work. Count the number of items in the to-do list generated by your plan—in most schools, they amount to enough responsibility to keep several full-time leaders at work. This penultimate chapter outlines some of the considerations you must take into account as you design the new curriculum, develop the skills of teachers, select the technologies, adjust the architecture, and modify the policies that will enable Education 3.0 at your school.

Few schools are set up to allow Sally to carry out the work pictured in her *Day in the Life*. They lack the technical infrastructure that made such activity possible; but more important, they have not developed the educational infrastructure that Sally needs. This includes the content of the curriculum, its materials, coordination, and assessment devices; the class scheduling and student grouping practices; the revised teaching methods and varied roles for the teacher; and the full integration of all of these with networked digital technologies. This chapter describes the nature of the educational infrastructure necessary to Education 3.0, and how it might be built.

CURRICULUM

The course of study for Education 3.0 is different from the curriculum in 2.0. Several differences are revealed in what this new curriculum does:

- Includes many skills and concepts not included in the old curriculum
- Leaves out some of the items covered in the old curriculum
- Is closely coordinated across subjects and between teachers
- Is available to students, managed, and tracked 100% online
- Requires the use of many technologies, including networked mobile devices
- Is confronted by students working along very different paths

Consider Sally's *Day in the Life*. While she ended up learning much of the same math, science, and literature as she would have under Education 2.0, she added to that many new skills in problem solving and analysis. And while she no longer spends much time learning to factor fourth-order polynomials, she spent quality time with statistical sampling. The content of the curriculum in Education 3.0 reflects the kinds of knowledge and skill she's more likely to need in her 21st century workplace.

Just about every topic Sally encountered in her day was connected directly to another subject area. Reading Thoreau's *Walden* while researching a local water-quality issue was not coincidental. Neither was the juxtaposition of statistics in math with water analysis in chemistry. The curriculum crafters at Sally's school meticulously designed a combination of group problems and formal lessons that covered all the bases and linked them with a synchronicity and complementarity far beyond anything we see in Education 2.0.

Such a curriculum requires nimble accessibility, sequencing, and scheduling, so that it can shift as necessary. Therefore it's all online, where it's easy for the teachers to find what they need, reorder the problems and lessons, and update as they go along. And easy for the students to access from anywhere, at any time, from any of the many networked information devices they use. Because it's online, it's easy to find just the lesson you need to solve the problem at hand; it requires no extra work on the part of the faculty to keep track of who is working on what, for how long, and with what results.

It's hard to find a printed textbook or reference book in an Education 3.0 school. But it's easy to find the course of study—just look on any of the computers, iPads, or other devices on the desks and in the pockets of the students and the faculty. A printed book does not keep track of who is reading what page, or how well they do on the end-of-chapter quiz. Nor can it help a struggling student decode and pronounce an unknown word, or link a complex phrase to a visual reference, as the digital books can. The online curriculum is essential to the efficiency and resiliency of student work in Education 3.0.

In addition to these computing, communication, and display devices are the data capture devices that the curriculum relies on. The data probe Sally used in the chemistry lab, the digital video camera her colleagues took to the bridge, even the violin that played the Bach riffs, formed integral aspects of the curriculum. These technologies enable the curriculum to interact directly with the facts on the ground, or under the water.

Curriculum Pyramids

A good way to understand the difference between the curricula of Education 2.0 and 3.0 is to picture a pyramid for Education 3.0 (see Figure 6.1) and invert the pyramid for Education 2.0 (see Figure 6.2). Think of it as a difference in where the curriculum starts.

In Education 3.0, the jumping-off point for study is a carefully crafted, worthwhile, interdisciplinary problem—a demand for students to apply many ideas and skills to a task at hand. Students start from the problem, which forms the tip of the pyramid. As they work through the problem, they are forced to work their way down to the rich depths of the pyramid, to learn the facts and concepts and skills they need to solve it. The problem seems pointed and focused, but underneath it lies an array of content that must be brought to bear in its solution. For an example of such a problem, read "The Watershed," a case study in Appendix B.

In Education 2.0, students begin at the wide end of the pyramid, absorbing (we hope) a mass of facts, concepts, and skills that may someday be applied to a worthwhile problem. Should they emerge from the bottom of the wide mass of the structure, and survive the descent to the point, they may be asked to apply what they have learned to a focused problem. But they seldom get this far.

In fact, in both eras of education the curriculum is formed of a myriad of pyramids. In Education 3.0, they are defined by the problems at their tips, with their bases made up of blocks from many different subject areas. In Education 2.0, the pyramids are defined by subject, all the math blocks in one, the literature blocks in another, many short and tipless, lacking a unifying focus. The net volume of both sets of pyramids is about equal, and consist for the most part of the same blocks. But the architecture is very different.

Turning Math Upside Down

Let's examine this concept of the upside-down pyramid with some examples from the mathematics curriculum.

In his 1623 book *The Assayer*, Galileo wrote,

> Philosophy is written in this grand book, the universe, which stands continually open to our gaze. But the book cannot be understood unless one first learns to comprehend the language and read the characters in which it is written. It is written in the language of mathematics, and its characters are triangles, circles, and other geometric figures without which it is humanly impossible to understand a single word of it; without these one is wandering in a dark labyrinth.[1]

FIGURE 6.1. Curriculum Pyramid in Education 3.0

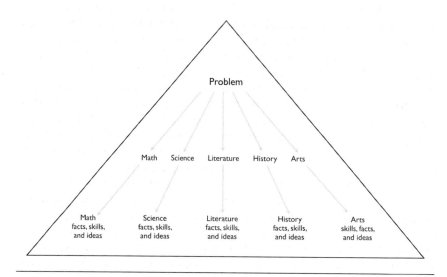

FIGURE 6.2. Curriculum Pyramid in Education 2.0

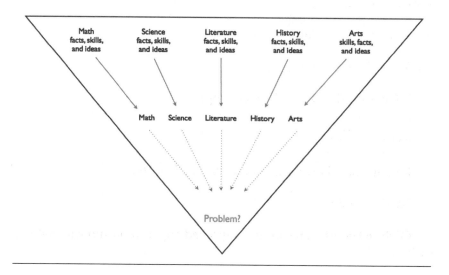

Later pundits have summarized this to "The book of nature is written in the language of mathematics." And indeed for the last 2,000 years humankind has been learning to read this book. Arab and Persian astronomers discovered the mathematics that determined the paths of the stars and invented a mathematical model to explain when heavenly bodies would move, appear, and disappear. Greek and Roman surveyors invented formulas and equations to help them bound and measure the extent of their empires. Philosophers of the enlightenment strove to explain and predict everyday occurrences through orderly systems of relationships.

Modern-day scientists and technicians made daily use of these discoveries and inventions when they harnessed the power of nuclear fission, predicted the path of the first rocket to the moon, and developed the GPS that tells you exactly where you are. Without mathematics, the very nature of the man-made world would not be what it is.

But somehow we have lost the sense of wonder and power that captivated and motivated the Arab astronomers, the Greek geometers, and the rocket scientists. We often teach mathematics as if it has no connection to nature. I watched some sixth graders at a top-flight school face a phalanx of long division problems—dividing decimals, on paper, with no explanation, no rationale for their connection with the real world. With glassy eyes and resigned countenances, they plowed through the 40 relentless problems and learned that math was a necessary chore with little application to or foundation in nature.

I worked with a community college that claimed only 10% of its freshmen were ready for college-level math, based on an entrance exam with 60 problems like these:

Factor the following:

$$6x^3 + 27x^2 - 105x =$$

What is the domain of the following?

$$f(x) = \sqrt{x - 7} + 2$$

Rewrite the following using only the sine function:

$$2\cos^2 x + \sin^2 x =$$

Of the 60 items on the exam, only 9 had any relationship with nature, such as:

A saline solution is 20% salt. How many gallons of water must be added to dilute the mixture to 8 gals of a 15% saline solution?

This severing of mathematics teaching and learning from nature and practicality is not a function of the college level. Look at the eighth-grade exam required by a major northeastern state of all its students. Most of the questions on the test—for which millions of students are being prepped every day—are like this:

What is the simplified form of the expression below?
$$8x^6 - 6x^3$$
$$2x^2$$

a. $4x^3 - 3$
b. $4x^4 - 3$
c. $4x^3 - 3x$
d. $4x^4 - 3x$

Of the 27 questions on the test, only 5 appear in any kind of an applied context. The questions we ask our students come out of the blue, with no relation to each other or to the original meaning of math. The math we teach and test in Education 2.0 bears little connection to nature, provides few practical applications, and lacks a sense of context.

Where's the drama of Galileo's dropping objects from the leaning tower? What happened to Newton's wonder at the fall of the apple? Where's the challenge of landing the rocket on the edge of the crater?

At an inner-city high school in the same state, the principal confronted the high number of his students failing math in their first year. "If only I could turn math upside-down, we could get them through it. Start with a practical problem, and learn the math as we work together to solve it. That's the way we want this school to work—but the math curriculum gets in our way."

The Common Core math standards now being proposed do no better at reviving the link to nature and practicality. In "Common-Core Math Standards: They Don't Add Up," Grant Wiggins shows how "there is not one word in the standards document about building curricula backward from rich, nonroutine, interesting, and authentic problems."[2]

The kind of math that this principal laments and the Common Core perpetuates is also not friendly to modern digital technologies. Students are not allowed to use common mathematical software tools when they take these tests, and the problems themselves are based on the kinds of paper-and-pencil tasks that mathematicians had to perform by hand before the advent of computers but seldom do any more. So there's little place for equation editors, graphing calculators, or geometric sketchpads in the teaching and learning of math in many schools. Even at schools where every student has a laptop in his backpack, math is often done with pencil and paper as it was a century ago.

How can we connect math back to its natural and practical origins and take full advantage of digital technologies as we teach and learn it? A few examples observed in forward-looking schools may suggest the right direction.

TENNIS BALL LAUNCHER

The tennis team doesn't need its practice ball launcher during fifth-period math. So the students set the angle, adjust the force, start the video recorder, and pull the lanyard. Pop, swoosh, and bop as the ball misses the trashcan target by 1.2 meters. Frame by frame they analyze the video clip, plotting the course of the ball with points on the cartesian plane laid over the video image. A pair of students downloads the coordinates of the points to a spreadsheet for further analysis, while another pair computes the initial velocity. "The closest curve-fit is parabolic, but the right half of the graph is off quite a bit from the perfect curve," reports the first pair. "We start off at 3 meters per second, but it drops pretty quickly as it reaches the top of the arc," reports the second.

BUNGEE JUMPING

Armed with videos of human bungee jumping, as well as a special apparatus they built in a corner of the gym, each small group of 12th-graders predicts the point at which the downward motion of the weight ceases. In order to do this accurately, they've had to learn to use differential equations, understand the acceleration of gravity (a second-order equation), and factor in the friction of the air. It's a complex prediction, with many possible paths to the truth. Each group plots its prediction with the graphing tools on their various laptops and mobile devices, runs and records the experimental apparatus, and reviews the digital video. The goal is to determine a mass that will stop falling just above the floor (for an example of such problems, see the NSF web site IDEA at http://www.idea.wsu.edu/Bungee/).

GREEN ROOF

The school roof needed replacement anyway, and the lowest bid came in at $153,000. The sixth graders are hard at work designing alternative roof systems more friendly to the environment than the rubber fabric proposed in the bid. One group designs a green roof, with rocks, grass, small bushes, and other natural features that conserve water and provide outdoor laboratory space for science experiments. They are developing their cost estimate. "We need a layer of gravel 2.5 centimeters deep across the entire eastern quadrant of the roof. How many square meters is that?" They do the calculations, multiplying and dividing decimals in rapid succession. They are thrown for a loop when their research finds that gravel is sold in cubic yards, not meters: more calculation, more math. "That puts us over $130,000, " reports the self-appointed accountant for the group.

How DIFFERENT FROM the flat page of long-division problems we began with. The approaches in these examples begin with a practical problem worth solving, one that requires certain math concepts and skills for its solution. The questions and the challenge are carefully designed by the teacher to require the learning and practice of the kinds of math the students need to learn. This is what the principal meant by turning the math curriculum upside down.

Have these students regained contact with the predictive and explanatory power of mathematics? Have they come to understand how it might help them get their work done, now and in the adult world? Have they shared a bit in the wonder and power that so impressed their ancient forebears? Have these schools moved toward Education 3.0?

GROUPING AND SCHEDULING

K–12 schooling in the Education 2.0 mode is wonderfully consistent in its grouping and scheduling of students and teachers all over the world. With few exceptions, a group of 25 students works in a room with a single teacher for sessions of a bit less than an hour, six or seven times a day. What's the reason for this? Is this the best way to accomplish our objectives?

In Education 3.0 students find themselves working at times in a small group of 5 or 6, at other times in a room with 25 of their peers, and often in a large group of over 100. The size of the group depends on what needs to be done. The work at hand may take 15 minutes, or a half hour, or 2 hours. The time allotted depends on what needs to be done. The curriculum crafters designed the size and duration of the groups to fit the task at hand, and to take advantage of the basic human needs for variety and community.

So we found Sally in the library for a 10-minute huddle with her five project teammates, then in the big lecture hall for a 60-minute demonstration from the online scientific expert to 150, then in the math classroom for a half-hour discussion with 25 others.

Some of her time was scheduled and directed for her, but some was allotted for self-directed activity. This self-direction is an important goal of the program; students earn more self-directed time as they work their way through their school careers. Sally enjoys much more freedom than her Education 2.0 counterparts, but this was earned gradually. And at the same time, Sally is more closely watched. All her time, every minute of the day, was effectively monitored by the communication devices she carried with her. The system knew where all the students were and what they were doing at all times. Sally's science teacher Mr. Bacon, the subject of *A Day in the Life of a Teacher* in Appendix A, was warned when several of his students wandered off-campus to the bridge to plant their data probe. And Max's teacher in *A Day in the Life of a Student: Elementary School,* also in Appendix A, gets a daily online report of the vocabulary words he is struggling with—with a copy to his parents. Time and activity, seemingly more open and loose, is in fact logged and tracked more closely in Education 3.0.

The development of self-direction is taken seriously in Education 3.0. It takes advantage of students' growing needs for self-identity, self-direction, and personal industry that often are given short shrift in Education 2.0. Capitalizing on the energy and industry of youth is a key component of Education 3.0.

The varied scheduling and grouping also enables a different role for the teacher, and permits a wider array of teaching and learning methods.

TEACHER DEVELOPMENT

The inversion of the pyramid described above calls forth some very different approaches to teaching. In the Education 2.0 pyramid, students visit the levels of each subject-pyramid block-by-block and row-by-row, beginning at the wide end. Seldom does their path form a logical sequence; seldom does it detour to a neighboring pyramid. At each block, the general method is the same:

- Present the content.
- Discuss or practice it.
- See if you've learned it.
- Put it aside in your mind.
- Go on to the next block.

And the specific techniques of teaching naturally limit themselves to this format. Teachers learn to present content, lead a discussion, and administer tests. These become the standard methods of instruction in the schools. Teaching centers around the lesson, a relatively short session in which a distinct block of content is set forth, exercised, and tested. In this routine, students often find themselves performing the same task as the person next to them. They seldom need to use resources from outside of the school. And there is little advantage offered by networked information technologies.

The general method of Education 3.0 looks more like this:

- Confront a worthwhile problem.
- Seek out ideas, facts, and skills that might help solve it.
- Gather, learn, and practice those ideas and skills.
- Apply them to the problem.
- Publish a solution.

The techniques for teaching in this context are quite different. Teachers spend their time articulating problems, pointing students to useful content, helping them learn and apply new ideas and skills, and teaching them how to publish their solutions. Teaching centers around the relatively long problem-solving process, in which an issue is introduced, attacked, and its solution published.

In this routine, students seldom find themselves performing the same task as the person next to them. They often rely on resources far beyond the walls of the school. And they simply could not get the work done without the help of digital networked information tools.

The general methods and routines of teaching and learning in Education 3.0 are more like the methods and routines of the modern laboratory and the workplace than they are like those of the school of Education 2.0. The way that time is used, the responsibility expected of the students, and the motivation for the work are less like school and more like work:

- Students spend less time on paper-and-pencil tasks and more time on computer-based tasks.
- Students seldom perform the exact same task as the student next to them.
- Students learn as much outside of the school building and day as they do inside.
- Learning relies on real-world computer and network tools, the same ones used in the world of research and business.
- Assignments require collaboration with other students, provide extra rewards for creative analysis, and expect innovative solutions.

LEADERSHIP

The curriculum described above, along with the other aspects of Education 3.0, do not develop of themselves. They are engendered by a well-thought-out vision, and implemented by a team of faculty and educational leaders. Leadership of such a school is a tough job. At the outset, it consists of:

- Building a new perception of learning and the role of school on the part of parents, students, teachers, and community. While business organizations, such as Cisco and Apple, and educational groups, such as the Partnership for 21st-Century Skills and Beyond the Basics, support leaders by providing a clear rationale for changing this perception, nonetheless, the kind of schooling pictured in the Day in the Life stories is far different from what the community is used to. Leaders must paint a clear picture of what the revised school looks like.
- Leading and supporting the faculty to build a new kind of curriculum, a new type of schedule, and a new way of working with students that supports this vision. Starting from a revised set of learning goals, the leadership must coach the faculty through the process of creating the new assignments, presentations, online resources, and facilities they'll need to open the school. And make sure they have the resources they need to do this work.
- Introducing the students and their parents to a new set of expectations, a vastly modified set of learning goals, and a new array of technologies. Getting them started in an Education 3.0 school requires more than a login password and a schedule; it calls for each student to rethink what school is about and how he or she works within it.
- Coordinating all of the aspects of Education 3.0, especially facilities and information technology, with the faculty and students so they combine as they should when they should.

As the Education 3.0 school settles in and grows, leadership remains critical as it:

- Nurtures faculty and students as they learn the ropes in a new environment. This involves monitoring their progress, listening to their concerns, and supporting their unanticipated needs.

- Ensures the full functioning of the technology infrastructure, encouraging users to point out ares of improvement, and communicating directly and often to the technology staff (which reports to and is evaluated directly by the school leadership).
- Monitors the perceptions of students, parents, and faculty of how well the school is achieving its goals, communicates with them frequently, and addresses their concerns.

There's more to building Education 3.0 than meets the eye. The transformed school depends on self-disciplined students, a creative faculty, a responsive set of technologies, and careful leadership to permit the kind of education we saw in the Day in the Life stories.

TECHNOLOGIES

Few of the educational leaders or teachers or students who participate in envisioning and building Education 3.0 are computer engineers. And yet their vision and their work depends so much on a set of technologies that the educators are not familiar with and don't know how they work. The shift a century ago from Education 1.0 to 2.0 was easier in part because the technologies were few and familiar to the principals and teachers: pens, paper, books, and chalkboards had been nearby and regularly used in education throughout their lifetimes. But most of the educators in the schools successful in moving to Education 3.0 need a crash course in digital networked technologies to make sense of the current shift. This section provides the beginning of such a course, through short briefings on the key technologies and how they apply to Education 3.0.

The Network

The lives we lead and the work we do in an Education 3.0 school or business or home would not be possible without the Internet, the network of networks. The network is the great enabler, the deliverer of possibilities, the basic infrastructure that lets us and our ideas flow across the planet. We can't see the network, though we use it every day. But we can imagine it. It's a rabbit warren of paths and tunnels under us all leading everywhere. It's a lattice or a matrix or a mesh or a grid putting the whole world on a coordinate plane. When it doesn't work for us, it's a disorderly tangle, a complex, or a maze. Some think it grows naturally like a nexus or a plexus or a web. Digital networks didn't exist when I went to school, but today no school could survive long without one.

Not all networks are created equal. The network that enables an international businessperson to appear in many places at once, or the students in Canada to interact daily with their peers in China, requires some careful planning and execution. To build Education 3.0, you need to understand the characteristics of a useful network—one that teachers and students can use to make their school a better place.

The networks that enable today's business and research and communication share some key characteristics. They are robust, reliable, flexible, open, and secure. They follow commonly accepted open standards, and they allow many types of devices to connect, using wires or radio signals. The network you build for your school in this step needs to share these characteristics.

Robust. The network needs to be strong enough to support what its users want to do. And these days, that means video, teleconferencing, and live meetings, as well as e-mail, databases, and documents. A traditional network designed to pass spreadsheets from one desk to another will not suffice or survive in the world pictured in your *Day in the Life*. The Education 3.0 network provides plenty of bandwidth, fast and unobtrusive routing of information to the right places, and a solid connection to the global backbone that connects us all. This essential strength provides the foundation for the services that follow.

Reliable. A network that goes down does not help its users move up. A useful network is designed with redundancies, backups, and alarms that prevent downtime. Competent people take responsibility to keep things running 24 hours a day, 7 days a week, and are on call when users experience difficulty. The Education 3.0 school monitors response time, downtime, and network performance, and reports these frequently to its leadership and its users. The digital information network is as important to the school as running water or electric power.

Flexible. The network managers in an Education 3.0 school seek out information on new network protocols, devices, and services that might be of use to students and teachers, frequently modifying the network to enable their use. The network allows devices, protocols, and services from a wide array of vendors and manufacturers, owned by students or by the school, to be connected and use its services. Like a successful species in a changing environment, the network adapts to the new developments in the world of information technologies. And it follows the basic Internet design principle of decentralization, so that a fault in one node or device does not bring the entire system to its knees.

Open. The network is designed to serve many purposes, traditional, present-day, and futuristic. It does not restrict the way its people use the network, except where safety or security is at risk. Network policies are set not to reduce the work of the network administrators, but to enhance the work of the teachers and students who use it. A useful network is a big tent, and welcomes all kinds of camels to nose around under it.

Standards-based. A useful network for an Education 3.0 school follows common standards agreed to by respected international organizations such as the Institute of Electrical and Electronics Engineers (see http://www.ieee.org/web/standards/home/index.html), the International Organization for Standardization (see http://www.iso.org/iso/standards_development.htm), the Moving Picture Experts Group (see http://www.chiariglione.org/mpeg/), and the World Wide Web Consortium (see http://www.w3.org/standards). The Internet is a worldwide resource, designed by its users through democratic deliberation; the standards for information exchange developed by these nonprofit, collaborative groups—public and open to all users—enable more useful networks than those built on secret proprietary protocols closed to other vendors.

Secure. Openness aside, evil exists in our world. A useful network is set up so as to prevent evildoers from disabling the network or stealing the private information of its users. Interestingly, the least secure networks are often those based on proprietary systems: Most of the viruses and hackers that we hear so much about exploit flaws in those secret schemes. Standards-based networks enjoy a wider array of security tools and experience far fewer evil disruptions.

Wired and –less. At least half the devices you saw in Sally's *Day in the Life* connected to the network by radio, not by cables. The smaller and more useful the device, the more likely it uses a wireless connection. The mobility that teachers and students need as they go about their work demands full open wireless access for all kinds of devices, as well as secure connections to the school network from home, such as that provided by a Virtual Private Network.

You may not need to appear in Katmandu at 2 o'clock, and you may not have shared a video clip with a colleague in China in quite a while. But you do need a solid, reliable, flexible, and open network in order to get your work done in an Education 3.0 school. And so do your students. Make sure the network that you build for your school stacks up against the characteristics described above.

Mobile Devices

Over the last decade, the miniaturization of communication and computing devices, the spread of wireless access to more places, and the online availability of academic information 24 hours a day, 7 days a week, from anywhere, togther have fomented a revolution in the way people do their work. Education 3.0 takes advantage of these developments.

In Education 3.0, we see students in the library, but not using the books—they are instead working with their project group to research a new idea from sources available only online. In Workplace 3.0 adults use their laptops to learn at a distance, enjoying full human interaction with the rest of the class. Young students go home with a bookshelf of new stories and texts on their iPod or iPad. College students review illustrated podcasts from their professors as they commute to campus. Students in the chemistry lab analyze reactions frame by frame through video shot with a mobile device. As the tools shrink smaller, the intellectual resources available to them grow broader.

On the table in front of me next to my iPod is a projector of the same size. I connect the two with a short cable and I can present slides to my seminar anywhere. And show student work. With one miniature device in each pocket, the portable professor can be quick on the draw, ready to shoot ideas onto the nearest wall.

The same iPod houses hundreds of books, from *The Odyssey* to *Paradise Lost* to *Programming with PHP/SQL*. It also holds video of Zeffirelli's *Romeo and Juliet*, music of Wagner's *The Flying Dutchman*, and dozens of podcast lessons in learning Chinese. Did I mention an animated school bus for beginning readers, along with an interactive number line for learning fractions?

Mobile devices have a place in every Education 3.0 plan that I have seen. Here's a summary of what you need to know to incorporate them wisely.

What are they? They are devices smaller than a bread box that let students learn. The list includes laptop computers, iPods, iPads, Kindles, Nooks, Sony Readers, small digital cameras, data probes, and some smart cell phones. The world is full of mobile digital devices, that's for sure; but few of them are used for learning. Most are used for entertainment and personal communication. But they harbor the potential to be used for serious academic purposes.

Why do we need them? These devices enable students to learn in new places, at new times, and in new ways. Students can carry materials for the entire curriculum in their pockets, and work with them in school, at home, on the bus, and in the park. Teachers can publish lessons in new formats, such as the podcast, which seem more suited to how today's students learn. Properly configured, some of these devices can add a new channel for teacher-student communication. And with some of these devices, students can more easily collect data and information and documentation from the field and bring it to school for analysis.

What do they do? They can store and display academic information in many formats: text, images, video, voice, music, graphics, maps. They can present exercises, quizzes, and tests that develop students' understanding. They can connect to the Internet for access to research. They can record text, voice, images, video, music, and real-world data. They can be turned into a graphing calculator, a geographic information display, or a response clicker. They can manage a student's schedule, contacts, classes, and assignments. They can communicate through e-mail or instant messaging. In fact, the best of today's mobile devices can do just about anything that a personal computer can.

How much do they cost? The least-expensive iPods and video cameras cost about $100; the most expensive smartphones cost $400. The most popular mobile device, the iPad, costs about $400. Only the Blackberry and the smartphones require a monthly fee; the others are free to use without recurring costs.

What are the system requirements? To use these devices in school you need a robust, standards-based, wireless network. Even more important (and sorely lacking in most schools), you need a robust, standards-based, online curriculum that can be displayed on the mobile devices and takes full advantage of their possibilities.

Who are the market leaders? Among young people, Apple's iPod, iPad, and iPhone products have captured the bulk of the market share. In some communities, upwards of 80% of high school and college-age people own one of these devices. Among working adults, the Blackberry has been the market leader among smartphones, but the iPhone and Android phones are catching up. Single-purpose devices such as the Kindle or the Sony Reader have yet to penetrate the mass market among students.

Why are mobile learning devices controversial in school? The answer to this question is beyond the scope of this book. Appendix D contains a list of articles that may help you to understand the current controversy.

Video Conferencing

Sally's day at school included an interactive video conference with an expert located far away. While this technology is used widely in business, its use for teaching and learning in schools is just beginning. You have many choices for web conferencing, from simple peer-to-peer systems like Messages and Skype (both free), to full-featured systems such as WebEx, eLuminate, and Adobe Connect. Define what you need to do to achieve your vision; then set your own specs for the video conferencing system you need.

To help you understand the scope and applicability of video conferencing in its many modes, we'll examine four scenarios drawn from actual experience in Education 3.0 schools. Perhaps one of these will help you build your vision of Education 3.0.

Distance Calculus

Only four students at Backwoods High School were interested in and qualified to take Advanced Placement Calculus this year. And since math teacher Louisa Laplace was out on maternity leave, no one was left to teach this AP math class. But across the state at Lone Mountain Academy, where enrollments have been dwindling, math teacher Francis Fourier is about to be reduced to an 80% schedule.

What they did. To solve the problem, the principal of Backwoods arranged for Fourier to conduct a calculus class three times a week using video conferencing. Fourier was in his classroom at Mountain Academy; the Backwoods students were in theirs, 250 miles away. Fourier plotted a curve on his computer using the CalcPad software; the students saw it displayed immediately on the SmartBoard in their classroom, as they heard their teacher's voice (and saw his face) explain the nature of the function he had entered. Students walked up one by one to the SmartBoard to plot new curves that extended the concept under study, as Fourier commented on their work (which he could see in real time on his computer, as he heard their voices).

On alternate days, Fourier held live office hours with his distant students, where students posed questions in text, as they showed their work on the SmartBoard. This method allowed the teacher to work with several students' individual problems at once, and to share his comments as necessary with one or many.

The role of video conferencing. Video conferencing in this situation serves as the channel for the students to communicate with their teacher at a distance, a channel which transmits just about all of the forms of interaction commonly found in a math classroom: presentation of information in text, diagrams, plots, curves, and equations by teacher or student; inspection and correction of student work by the teacher; question and answer sessions with the entire group or with individual students. Video conferencing software such as WebEx provides an array of technologies that allow the course to carry on even though teacher and students are separated by a long distance.

How they did it. The Backwoods School District licensed the web conferencing software, and selected a computer in the math classroom to serve as the school-based end of the communication. Because the computer came with a built-in video camera, microphone, and speaker, no hardware configuration was necessary—and no software needed installation. They simply launched their web browser, connected to the web conferencing server, and all was taken care of. Any software needed was automatically provided through the online connection. This computer was already connected to the SmartBoard, so all was ready.

The teacher at Mountain Academy added a webcam and headphones to his laptop, fired up his browser. They were ready to communicate. The staff at Backwoods connected to the web conference server, entered their password, and set up a regularly scheduled meeting every Monday, Wednesday, and Friday at 10:00 a.m. The system automatically e-mailed the time, URL, and password of the meeting to Francis Fourier at Mountain Academy.

At the appointed hour, both the computer in the math classroom, and the one in Fourier's lap, connected to the meeting URL, entered the password, and joined the meeting. When Fourier wanted the students at Blackwoods to see a plot on a graph, he clicked the presenter button on his computer, and told it to display his CalcPad window to the meeting. If the students didn't understand a certain point on the curve, they could move a pointer on their own computer as they asked their question. Fourier could see the pointer and respond accordingly. If he wanted to see the students' work, he clicked them into presenter mode and watched as their work appeared on his screen as they explained their results over the headphones.

EXPERT INTERVIEW

Mrs. Woolf's English class at Bloomsbury High School in rural Steinbeck, California, had developed what they and their teacher thought was a novel way to stage the scene in Shakespeare's Hamlet where the protagonist famously un-declared his love for Ophelia. It's a key scene in the play, and one which is normally staged to portray a helpless, innocent Ophelia and a rude, wisecracking Hamlet on the verge of madness. Their version in contrast shows a cruel and complicit Ophelia toying with Hamlet and driving him to madness.

With the help of extensive online research, the students located Laertes Guildenstern, the world's expert on Hamlet, who had recently published an authoritative exegesis of this very scene. He kindly agreed to correspond with the class by e-mail to answer their questions. Intrigued by their ideas, this scholar-in-residence at the Folger Shakespeare Library in Washington, D.C., asked to see their scene so that he might analyze it further.

The cross-country analysis was accomplished through web video conference. A video camera and microphone focused on the school stage connected to a computer connected to the video conference server. At the other end, Guidenstern and a few of his colleagues watched the scene unfold on the big screen in the Folger's conference room. When it was finished, he asked the students where they got their ideas. They explained how their staging had arisen from a discussion in class about gender stereotyping in literature. He asked them to wait a moment while he went into the rare book section of the archives, as they discussed the finer points of the scene with the other Folger scholars.

Returning to the conference room, Guidenstern placed a page of scene directions and drawings from a 1735 document found in a London theater onto the scanner at the Folger. As it displayed on the SmartBoard to the students in Steinbeck, they and their teacher savored the similarities to their own version. The online discussion continued for the rest of the afternoon.

The role of video conferencing. Web conferencing facilitated a scholarly exchange and a discovery that probably would not have occurred without easy real-time multimedia communication over long distances. It allowed hard-working students in a rural school to work on an educational project with experts, separated by a continent but united in their interest in Shakespeare's work. Web video conferencing makes it easy for the outside expert to connect—they simply point their browser to a URL and the video conference server does the rest. So it's easy for the scholar or the speaker to sit at his or her desk and spend a few moments with Bloomsbury High School students. And both sides can bring to bear whatever media they need to tell their story, from video to text to drawings to images.

How they did it. After licensing the video conferencing service, the leadership of Bloomsbury High School encouraged the faculty to reach out to resources and expertise that would enhance teaching and learning. Teachers and students learned how to use the Internet to find out who the experts were and then track them down, usually by e-mail. Most of their contacts did not mind being used in this way, as long as the school made it easy for them and respected their time and schedule.

Once they found the expert they needed, they scheduled a video conference and made sure the expert had what was necessary to connect. A squad of tech-savvy students calling themselves the VC Techs contacted Guildenstern in advance; he put them in touch with the technical people at the Folger Library, and together they configured the necessary equipment for a two-way audio, video, and whiteboard session.

The session itself consisted of a conversation between two groups: students and their teacher at Bloomsbury High School and Laertes Guildenstern and his colleagues at the Folger Library. They could see and hear each other, exchange documents, and act out a scene from the play. In fact, as the scene progressed, the scholars at Folger used the web conferencing text chat function to comment silently on what they were seeing and to pose questions to the students—those not acting in the scene were monitoring the chat window. And the archive of the chat became an important document for further learning.

BORDERLESS BUTTERFLIES

As the winner of the annual Undergraduate Research Award at Monarch College, Dana Plexipus was funded to travel in late August through early November to the Mariposa Monarca Biosphere Reserve in Tlalpujahua, Mexico, where she would measure the migrating butterfly population using a new digital imaging technique that she had invented. Her method allows the automated estimation of the number of butterflies based on photos taken at periodic intervals in specific locations, whose pixels undergo image analysis with Dana's software algorithm. (Since they are monarch butterflies, the software counts the proportion of orange pixels in the photo to estimate the number of insects.) The result is a butterfly count that is twice as accurate as the human counters previously used in migration research.

The trouble is, Dana is required by Monarch College to take the Advanced Statistics Seminar, Math 499A, in order to earn her degree in biology (and to qualify for graduate school). Math 499A, a seminar limited to 12 students, is taught only in the fall semester, when the butterflies are migrating and Dana is scheduled to be in Mexico.

What they did. Professor Bayes, who has led the Advanced Statistics Seminar for 34 years at Monarch College, sets up his laptop at the end of the seminar table opposite his chair. He has set up a recurring video conference every Tuesday from 2:00 until 5:00 p.m. to coincide with his seminar. With the laptop open on the table, he can see across to the screen, as can the other students at the table. At 1:55 every Tuesday, he connects the browser to the video conference, and turns up the volume. The laptop, with built-in video camera, microphone, and speakers needs no further configuration.

As the rest of the seminar students wander in, they see Dana's face appear on the display of the laptop, and hear her plaintive "Is anyone there?" voice. One of the students enlarges the image so that Dana fills the screen. Students lean over the video camera to greet her and ask how the research is going. At 2:05 Bayes gets the seminar started with a discussion of the sampling strategies that each student is using in his or her data collection. They respond around the table. Dana chimes in at her turn, with voice and video.

Dana is sitting at the Internet Café in Tlalpujahua, peering into the video camera in her laptop and making her report. The other customers are fascinated with what she's doing. She can display equations on the whiteboard, show sample photos to the rest of the class and zoom into the key details, pixel-by-pixel. It costs her the equivalent of U.S. $30 to spend the 3 seminar hours each week using the café's broadband connection, the only one in town. But it's worth it—already what she's learned in the seminar about sampling error has helped her to modify her image-processing algorithm for more accuracy.

The role of video conferencing. Web conferencing makes it possible for Dana to attend an important college course even though she's thousands of miles away. Except for touching the other students, there's nothing educational she can't do through her digital connection to the seminar. She sees all that's going on, she listens, she speaks, she shows her work, she asks and responds to questions. In the eyes and ears of her professor, she's a full participant in the course. His only accommodation to her special needs is to fire up his laptop once week and save a place for her at the seminar table.

How they did it. The college licensed the video conferencing software, made the faculty, staff, and students aware of its possible uses, and provided technical support to get them started. Once shown how to schedule a meeting and set up his laptop, Bayes was on his own each week to initiate the connection and bring Dana into the seminar. the same was true at

Dana's end: She simply pointed her browser to the meeting URL, entered the password, and she was at the table. She learned from the video conferencing web site how to do some of the more interesting applications, such as putting her images on the whiteboard, or displaying her equations to the class. Since these functions are built into the video conferencing software, she needed no special configuration or engineering assistance.

Special Ed Staffing

After 6 months with his new cochlear implants, Jacob was ready to learn for the first time in a regular classroom with a generalist teacher and non-hearing-impaired students. Getting everyone ready for this transition was no easy task. Jacob's specialist in Milwaukee, his pediatrician in Davenport, his teacher and principal at Rock Island Elementary, and the Special Education Coordinator at the Central Office, all had to work together to make Jacob's mainstreaming a success.

Arranging a meeting of all involved was next to impossible, and things were not progressing well until they started using video conferencing. Now they are meeting once a week, just for a half hour, but it has made quite a difference. Today's meeting will last longer, because they have added an acoustic architect from Chicago to the group. After Jacob's first visit to his new classroom, everyone noticed how noisy it was, and even with the implants Jacob was not hearing as well as he did at home or in the doctor's office.

The architect asked Jacob's teacher to take him first on a video tour of the room. At the architect's direction, she pointed and zoomed the video camera at the windows, the ceiling, the floor, the doors, the desks, the chairs. All this video was being saved in an archive by the video conferencing software so that the architect could examine it more closely later. Next the architect asked everyone else in the meeting except the teacher to switch off their microphones so he could concentrate on the acoustic environment of the classroom. This meeting was specifically scheduled during the school day so as to capture a typical noise level.

It was clear to everyone why Jacob was having trouble hearing. The classroom was alive with extraneous noise. A rattling ventilation fan, metal chair legs scraping on an asphalt tile floor, buzzers and announcements from the intercom, other classes talking as they moved through the hall, squealing chalk, all reflected and amplified by the hard floor, cement walls, glass windows, and smooth metal ceiling.

In the discussion that followed when all had switched their microphones back on, the recommendations were clearly understood by the teacher (who would implement some of them), the principal (who would coordinate the necessary modifications to the room), the custodian (who was brought into the meeting by the principal as soon as she saw where things were heading), the special ed coordinator (who would budget for the necessary expense), and the specialist (who was pleased to have the problem identified). It was a short list: In the short term, put tennis balls on all the chair and table legs while waiting for the carpet to be installed during vacation week; put insulation around the door to the hall; install sound-absorbing panels on the walls and ceiling; replace the ventilation fan; switch from chalkboard to whiteboard; put drapes over the windows; and route the intercom through a small speaker on the teacher's desk.

The role of video conferencing. Web conferencing enabled what is called a *staffing* on Jacob—a meeting of a group of people involved in his care and education, designed to help him overcome his handicaps. Without video conferencing, a staffing such as the one described above would have been almost impossible to arrange. Web conferencing made it possible to bring to bear a range of expertise from many different locations to focus on a single problem in real time. And it enabled many foci: video, audio, images, background sounds, voices. It allowed a specialist many hundreds of miles away to make a virtual visit to Jacob's classroom in the company of other specialists. And all of them could confer to solve the problem.

How they did it. The school district licensed the video conferencing system, and briefed administrators on its possibilities. The Special Education Coordinator quickly recognized its ability to help conduct the all-important staffings required by state and federal law. She scheduled the meetings on the video conference calendar, which sent out automatic reminders to the participants. She suggested the teacher connect the school's good video camera to the computer to give a better-quality image for the architect's analysis, and better audio.

She found that it was easy for the outside experts to connect, and that the meetings went faster online than they did in person. No one traveled; all worked from their classrooms or offices where the necessary resources stood close at hand.

Online Learning

It seems a lot easier to learn in a classroom than online. In the classroom, you simply sit while the teacher talks and you learn. There's not much to worry about. Occasionally, they ask you a question, but for the most part your responsibility is to take a test at the end of the term. It's comfortable, we've been learning this way for years, everyone knows how it's done.

In contrast, online learning seems uncomfortable. You sit alone on the line, not sure what you're supposed to do, with no one expecting you to show up, no one standing there telling you what to do. You're on your own. Education 3.0 relies on this new kind of learning, so you need to prepare yourself to succeed at it.

GROWTH OF ONLINE LEARNING

The biggest growth in online learning is occurring in offices and factories and laboratories across the globe, as corporations move their training and development programs from the classroom to the computer. Companies such as Cisco Systems have developed a university-sized array of online courses and updates for its employees, which they are expected to use to learn new things.

Online learning is also growing on campus. The number of college students taking their coursework online rather than in the classroom has doubled in the last 5 years. From Stanford to Yale to Duke to Rappahannock Community College to MIT, professors are learning to teach, and students are learning to learn, in a new environment that's quite different from the lecture hall.

Even at home, more of us are going online to learn things we want or need to know to help us in our everyday lives. For example, baking the bread for the evening meal became my responsibility one day. I had not a clue how to do it. So I went online and found a course in Bread-Baking for 4-Year-Olds ("No knead bread: So easy a 4-year-old can make it" at http://steamykitchen.com/blog/2007/09/10/no-knead-bread-revisited).   In words and pictures, it led me through the process of mixing the dry ingredients, adding the water, rising, rising again, and baking. And they liked it! The proof is in the pudding, you might say.

REASONS FOR GROWTH

So it's all around us, and growing quickly, as the Internet reaches more desktops and laptops and iPads with multimedia materials and illuminating lessons. A recent report by the Sloane Foundation documents this growth, who's leading it, and the reasons for it (see http://www.sloan-c.org/publications/survey/staying_course). Why this tremendous growth in online learning in so short a time? We can find several reasons.

More opportunities to learn. Even though your school is not large enough to offer Calculus or Chinese or Computer Science, your students can take these courses anyway and get credit for them by studying online.

An online connection allows them to learn with an expert in Alberta or with fellow students in Albania, without leaving the classroom.

More learning styles. People learn in different ways. Sometimes students learn best by reading the text, skimming for the main idea or working slowly through a dense argument. At other times they learn best while listening to someone explain it to them in a calm and patient voice. And there are some concepts, especially in science, that they can learn only if they can see them in action. Online learning allows a student to choose which method is best for the situation at hand.

More learning modes. Sometimes students learn best all by themselves. At other times they need to bounce ideas off a small group of trusted peers. And some ideas are best learned in a large group where they're all online and can help each other work their way through the material. Online courses let them choose the mode that's best right then.

Self-paced. Sometimes, when they're in a state of flow, students plow right through the subject, learning deeply and quickly whatever is put in front of them. At other times they need to work slowly, going back and forth over the same idea many times before they get it. Online courses let them learn at their own pace.

Self-correcting. After studying for a while, students like to test themselves to see if they've learned anything. Online courses often include frequent self-correcting quizzes that let students assess their progress and even guide them along when they get the wrong answer. This is much more effective than waiting for the midterm to see if they're learning anything.

Cross-referenced. In the classroom with 25 others, it's hard to delve deeper or check out alternative views. But online, students are connected to a World Wide Web of cross-references, details, original sources, illustrations, and examples that range far beyond what's available in the school library. So their learning can be enriched by a wide array of resources.

Times Have Changed

When you went to school, most of the time you sat in class, led by the teacher. Once in a while you did independent research in the library, and some amount of homework in the evening. Nonetheless, the bulk of the time was spent sitting and listening.

But the world has changed. In the workplace today, people spend very little time sitting and listening. They are online communicating with their customers, or taking an online course to improve themselves, or working with a small group of coworkers to solve a problem. If we want school to prepare people for this new workplace, we need to better match the learning modes to the real world.

And if we want school to prepare our students for college, we need to understand that college students spend only about 12 hours a week in a classroom—about 15% of their waking hours. The rest is spent learning online, or working independently in the library, or studying with fellow students. The more that high schools can match this style, the better prepared they'll be for college.

Does Online Learning Work?

Not for everybody. While online learning has enabled millions of people to excel who are not good classroom learners, a few folks are frustrated. They can't seem to concentrate on what they need to do unless someone is right there giving them directions. People who have succeeded online say that the experience helped them build self-reliance and self-confidence: They were better able to figure things out for themselves. Others extol the flexibility of online learning, letting them study whenever and wherever they want, moving as slowly or as quickly as they need to, and assessing their own progress. All agree that the online approach helped them develop time-management skills, the ability to discipline themselves to set time aside to get up and do what needs to be done. They explain that they have, like Sally, taken over their own learning plan: They don't wait for someone to tell them what do learn and when, and they don't learn merely to please the teacher—they learn to improve themselves. This can only help them in their future lives.

Conditions for Success

How can we set things up in our Education 3.0 so that we succeed at learning online? First of all, we need to build in an environment that makes it easy to work online. A good computer or mobile device with a solid Internet connection for every student and teacher is essential. It helps to have people nearby who can assist you through the tough parts.

What we need to remove from the Education 3.0 environment, both at school and at home, is the television. This ubiquitous appliance is anathema to learning. It cries for attention, it flashes visual drivel designed to interrupt your train of thought, and has proven itself to be a detriment to academic achievement. Start a parent education campaign to *Turn it off*. Better yet, *Put it in the closet*. One of the reasons Sally succeeds in life is her reclaiming 6 hours per day from the boob tube that she uses for learning.

Music is another matter. Certain types of music have been shown to provide a calming background for study that drowns out the interruptions of the world around us and enables us to concentrate on our learning. Music without lyrics works best. For Sally, the predictable repetitions of Bach or the soft strings of Sibelius help her get her work done.

No matter where our students are or what they are listening to, it's time that matters. Time is of the essence. Unless students learn to manage their own time, they will not succeed at online learning (or the many other aspects of Education 3.0). At birth we are granted by our creator 3 score and 10 years; it's how we spend that gift that determines our worth and our success. Set a time for learning, start promptly, and stick to it until the task is complete.

Finally, when students have worked through a set of online materials, they need to have someone to talk with about what they have learned. A parent, a spouse, a good friend, or a fellow student can help them reflect on what they have uncovered. This consolidates learning and puts it into a social context.

ONLINE COURSE QUALITY

Education 3.0 depends in large measure on learning that takes place online. As schools move in this direction, they are learning how to design online courses that work well in the new learning environment. This section of the book summarizes some of the factors, both technical and pedagogical, that make for high-quality online learning.

Let's look at four vignettes that may have been overheard in the hallways of a school near you. All of these include examples of online learning. As you read them, decide how you would rank them in terms of quality? Why?

1. Next week's class will take place online. You'll find all the materials you need posted on Blackboard. The objective for next week is to understand the leading psychological theories of children's moral development, and be able to apply them to what goes on in your classroom. First, you'll read a concise introduction to the three main theories and then a short classroom-based research study based on one of the theories recently published in Child Development. You'll take a short quiz to ensure you've under-

stood what you've read; then you'll enjoy my 10-minute illustrated podcast that relates these theories and research to daily life in the classroom. After that you'll watch video clips of moral discussions in two classrooms and be asked to identify which students show which stages of development. Finally, you'll record a short moral discussion that you conducted in your own classroom, analyze your own students' stages of moral reasoning, and send me the results.

2. No class meeting next week. Since the Yankees are playing the Mets in the World Series on Wednesday, all the subways will be crowded and it will take you forever to get here. So instead you'll do some work online. Read the next chapter in the textbook, then post your comments to the discussion board on our learning management system (LMS). If you have any questions, send them to me on e-mail. Write a one-page summary of the chapter and bring it to class 2 weeks from now.

3. The magic of technology enabled us to record every lecture in this course last semester. The lectures are all posted online, with synchronized PowerPoint slides and lots of graphics. Go to the Moodle site and you'll see all 14 of them. We also recorded a different section meeting each week, and these too are all online in living color. As a substitute for our regular class meeting next week,watch those videos, then complete the 50-question multiple-choice test you'll find on Blackboard that will test your knowledge of the subject matter.

4. Next week your goal is to learn about the different economic systems in British overseas colonies in the second half of the 18th century, and to understand how they contributed to varying forms of political organization. Each group of three students has been assigned one colony; what you need to do is to complete the first draft of your illustrated analysis and send it to me by Friday. I expect that your group will meet together face-to-face at least once during the week and have another meeting as an online chat. Your final report must include references to at least four of the readings that I have posted on Blackboard; it must also include information from at least two original sources that you locate on your own. Your illustrations should include at least two contemporary images such as paintings, etchings, artifacts, or maps. I'll assess your work based on the rubric posted on Blackboard that includes concepts from both political science and economics.

As more and more teachers move to include online learning in their courses, we need to look closely at what works and what doesn't, what's acceptable and what's not, and what's a best practice and what is to be avoided. The University of Phoenix, a recent (founded in 1976, online in 1989) and fast-growing institution of higher education, has been called on the carpet recently for shoddy practices in online education, for lowering academic standards for the sake of convenience. Faculties all over the world are asked to determine the quality of online courses compared with traditional classroom-based instruction. How do educators distinguish the gold from the dross?

First, we must determine how much the online course is worth, compared to the traditional course delivered in the classroom. We might arrive at this by considering three measures: time, work, and learning.

Time. We have for centuries described our courses in terms of credits and time: a three-credit course meets 3 hours a week for 15 weeks. So 45 hours of class time is worth three credits; and we expect that class time is complemented by the student with independent reading and writing and lab time. To follow this tradition, we would analyze online learning in terms of how many hours students devote to it: a three-credit online course should consume perhaps 75 hours of a student's time (45 class hours + 30 hours for homework). As we look at an online course, we can estimate how much time it would take a student to complete each assignment, and use that to judge its quality. So we might expect a three-credit online course to include 75 assignments, each taking an hour to complete. And for atypical online weekly session, we might expect 5 hours of work by the student. We can even set up our learning management system to track how long each student spends with each online assignment, if we want to be sticklers about it.

Work. But time may not be the best measure. What we want to see is student work: The amount of work they accomplish in an online course should equal or exceed what they do in a classroom-based course. Following this approach, we would look for students to absorb the material presented in the weekly lecture, read the 50 or so pages of text normally assigned in that week, plus complete the assigned lab work. Some will get this work done in 3 hours; for others it might take 6. Of course, they need to turn the work in each week so we know they've done it. So we'd measure the quality of an online course by how much work is involved on the student's part, and make sure it's equivalent to the work required in classroom-based courses.

Learning. But it's not the work they do that matters, it's what they learn. So perhaps the best way to evaluate an online course is to point the students to all the materials they need to cover, and then give them a test or paper to write that shows whether or not they learned it. With this approach, we need not concern ourselves with the means of education, only the ends. We would make sure that the amount of learning that occurs in the online course meets or exceeds what's learned in the face-to-face version. So we don't concern ourselves much with the hours or the activity, but concentrate on the assessment. As long as they pass the test, they get credit, whether it's online or off. We need only look at the quality of the assessment, and its evaluation rubric, to judge the online course.

ALL OF THESE approaches have merit; most of us combine all three as we examine the new digital offerings that come across our display screens. All share the weakness of comparison with a suspect standard: Are we sure that our current classroom-based practices represent the most effective forms of learning? Perhaps it would be better to develop a comprehensive approach to describing and judging an online course. In our work with hundreds of designers, teachers, and students of online courses, we have found that successful courses pay careful attention to four elements bjectives, exploration, wrestling, and production. If any of these are missing, or weak, the course does not pass muster.

Objectives. You'd be surprised at what's offered up as objectives on the syllabi of faculty members who teach online. Here are a few examples:

- To talk about the influence of deconstructionism on the work of street artists in the Paris Commune of 1968
- To cover the material in chapters 15–18 of the text, *Modern Astrophysics*
- To deal with the four main theories of child development as they apply to language learning disabilities

And you'd be surprised at how many online courses and sessions make no mention at all of what is to be learned: They state neither goals nor objectives nor expectations. They simply post a collection of readings or activities. To be acceptable, an online course needs, as any course, a set of objectives, stated in terms of what the student is expected to learn. Here are some samples:

- Analyze e-commerce sites according to classic business principles and new concepts of e-commerce

- Design and program a prototype e-commerce site that follows solid business principles and digital design concepts
- In this section of the course, you will learn to: define language and describe its rule systems; discuss the biological and environmental aspects of language; evaluate how language and cognition are linked; describe how language develops in children; and summarize the features of African American English

This second set of objectives is more useful because it explains what the student will be able to do when they finish the online session. And these kinds of objectives make the form of assessment of student learning self-evident, the importance of which we will soon see.

Exploration. Unless the student thinks some new thoughts in the course of his online experience, then there's no education. So every online session or course must cause the student to explore new materials, confront new ideas, develop new concepts, or practice new skills. A summary of the familiar, or a rehash of the obvious, no matter how slickly it's presented, does not suffice. And the more that this exploration involves different forms of communication—reading, writing, images, video, case study, simulation, and so forth—the more likely it is to provoke thinking. An online session or course that lets students stay in their own intellectual back yard and does not require foreign exploration doesn't make the grade.

Wrestling. Without dissonance, the resolution does not satisfy. The new ideas that students explore in the online course must be carefully crafted to provoke questions in the student's mind, engender cognitive conflict, or afflict the comfortable prejudice. The student must wrestle with the new ideas or new skills in order to understand them. So we should look for online assignments that call for comparison, contrast, taking the wrong side of an issue, practicing a technique that you've never tried before. An online session that simply expects students to remember and repeat, or skim and summarize, would not meet this criterion.

Production. In many of the online courses that I have seen, the student is asked to produce nothing; she needs simply to read, watch, listen, and perhaps discuss. But unless a student produces something that proves that she has mastered the objectives, how will we know it worked? So for each objective, there must be a production, a piece of work that the student creates that provides evidence of learning. It can be as simple as a multiple-choice test, as familiar as a two-page paper, or as complex as a group podcast. To qualify for approval, an online course or session must call for an assessment of its objectives, produced by each student.

Go back and look at the four vignettes printed at the beginning of this section, and analyze each in terms of the three comparisons (time, work, learning) and four elements (objectives, exploration, wrestling, and production). Which of them pass the quality test? Use Table 6.1 to record your results.

Learning Management Systems

Sally's school, and most that move toward Education 3.0, find that they need a technology called a *learning management system* (LMS) to enable them to achieve their goals. Few of them actually manage learning. What most of them do is allow teachers to post their course materials, and students to access them, online. They are essentially big databases running on your server that manage who has access to what content: who can post it there, and who can look at it. Many of them also keep track of who has looked at what, score simple quizzes, and allow students to submit assignments online.

LMSs do not provide content: That's done by the teacher, or by license from a major publisher, all of whom provide their textbook content in formats to run on the most popular LMSs.

Why do I need one? It makes things easier for teachers and students, and does away with piles of books and papers. Most colleges in the United States employ LMSs, as do an increasing proportion of high schools. An LMS can provide flexibility in when and how students learn, and open the door to online courses.

What can LMSs do? Many vendors are ready to sell you an LMS, or you can make your own. All of them can do the following things:

- Allow teachers to post learning materials online
- Organize things course by course
- Manage student login and registration into courses
- Allow teachers to create simple quizzes
- Allow students to turn in assignments online
- Keep track of who has done what

In addition, the more developed LMSs can do other things like these:

TABLE 6.1. Results of quality test

Time	Work	Learning	Objectives	Exploration	Wrestling	Production
Example 1						
Example 2						
Example 3						
Example 4						

- Allow teachers to post more complex content, such as video and animation
- Allow teachers to create more complex tests and quizzes
- Provide automated online gradebooks for teachers and students
- Provide discussion boards, chat rooms, and virtual classrooms
- Manage instant messaging and e-mail among the school community
- Manage subgroupings of students within a course
- Manage lunch count, attendance, and room access (with swipe cards)

How much do they cost? The most expensive proprietary systems will cost upwards of $100,000 per year for a large school and with all features. The least expensive open-source LMSs will cost you only the time of your staff to install and configure them.

What are the system requirements? All require a robust network infrastructure within the school, a Unix server, and a mainstream database. All are web-based and allow multiplatform clients. Some provide interfaces for mobile devices. All work better in an environment where each student owns his own computer or compatible mobile device.

Who are the market leaders? Among proprietary systems, Blackboard is the big player; among open-source LMSs, Moodle is the leader. Below those, many smaller companies are in the business of selling and maintaining LMSs for schools. Sakai is gaining a following among universities. And iTunesU, while not a fully featured LMS, is being used by many schools to distribute multimedia learning materials on campus, aimed at both computers and mobile devices.

Podcasting

Sally begins her trip to school listening to two podcasts, one about water pollution and the other about Thoreau's *Walden*. Most of the Education 3.0 plans include a large measure of student work with podcasts, those produced by their own teachers as well as others from outside sources. What do you need to know about podcasting to build Education 3.0?

Schools have produced some *Day in the Life* stories that show iPods strapped to the arms of students so they can listen and learn as they as jog, and others that involve students downloading the *New York Times* to their iPads so they can read the news during study break. Still others show how a student subscribes to his math teacher's podcast so he can prepare for tomorrow's quiz or how students use smartphones to snap a picture of their teacher's physics experiment and send it to their computers via e-mail. Students in Education 3.0 enjoy the portability of their digital resources in ways that none of us dreamed about as few as 5 years ago.

How are teachers in Education 3.0 taking advantage of this new channel into their students' minds? Millions of students own iPods and iPads, treating them as constant companions and digital drop boxes. More than simply a way to listen to music and watch movies, the portable devices have become a depository for e-mail messages, a storage space for software, and a location for listening to lectures at leisure. So it's natural that their teachers seek to find ways to make educational materials available on these new and highly competent portable multimedia devices.

As I help teachers implement Education 3.0, I have uncovered some interesting approaches to using podcasting for teaching and learning. I have heard science podcasts that sound like comedy sketches, and I have watched endless video archives of lackadaisical literature lectures. I have watched students eagerly download morsels of math instruction with clever slides and nice narration to prepare for tomorrow's test. As your teachers think about the possibilities of this portable medium, encourage them to consider the three main areas:

- Context
- Content
- Quantity

Context. The ubiquity of the iPod stems from its excellence as a music player. It was designed to be easy to carry with headphones so you could listen anywhere, with simple controls that you can work with one finger. People use their iPods on bikes, beaches, trains, cars, sidewalks, park benches, and lecture halls. They listen for a few minutes or a long stretch, depending on where they are and what else they are doing. They listen or watch alone—only one person at a time in most instances. What they listen to habitually is music, so they are conditioned to audio experiences that last about 4 minutes, the duration of a typical popular song.

So the first question for the teacher to ask is where and how and why the students will be using the podcast they plan to produce. Will they be on the subway reviewing 2-minute key concepts lessons for an upcoming quiz? Or will they be in the library listening to the hour-and-a-half lecture they missed because of football practice? Will they be in a place suitable to viewing video or images and have the equipment that can handle this? Will they have a few minutes as they walk between classes to let your voice enter their minds through the little white ear buds? Or will they schedule an iPod study group and all listen together in a digital all-nighter?

The podcasting context for high school students may be quite different from the contexts for grad students or middle schoolers. The nature of the context will determine what your first podcasts should look like. It's easier to achieve success if you match the style and purpose of your podcast to the context that most iPod-using students are familiar with.

Content. We think of the iPod as a music player, so we assume that an academic podcast should be first of all an audio experience. But a podcast may contain images, text, and video as well as sound. This means you may use printed words, diagrams, photographs, animation, and film clips in your podcasts, as well as voice. So your first consideration is to select the content that best serves your purposes. An art historian may find images to be quite useful, a musician may need to include symphonic recordings, a math teacher may use diagrams to make a point, and a geographer may be partial to maps. A podcast may include any and all of these. It may also include text. Podcasts may include a lyrics channel that contains the text of the narration, word for word.

A teacher's choice of the type of content to use will stem from what material is available already and how much time there is to produce it. It's easier to turn an existing video clip into a podcast than to produce a brand new one. It's easier to modify a slide show you already have into a podcast than to build one from scratch. It's easier to base a podcast on a proven story you have told over and over than to write a brand-new original script. So examine your photo collection, your lecture slides, your class notes, and your video library for appropriate source material before you plan your podcast.

But don't fall into the trap of simply copying an existing lecture and pasting it into a podcast. The context for consuming a podcast is quite different from that of the lecture hall. Think instead about adapting the content of a lecture—images, key points, examples—into the shorter forms more appropriate to the portable medium. Split the lecture into three or four podcasts. Record your talk in a style that's more person-to-person.

You will find that certain types of podcasts are easier and quicker to produce than others:

- *Audio podcast—sound only.* Easiest to produce. At its simplest, you click the record button in GarageBand, speak your piece, and save it to iTunes or iWeb. And it will work on all iPods and iPads and on many MP3 players, as well as on a Web page or in a course management system such as Blackboard.

- *Enhanced podcast—sound plus pictures.* A bit more difficult to produce, but perhaps more useful. Just drag the artwork into the track in GarageBand, and slide them around to sync with your voice. Most existing images—including slides from Keynote or PowerPoint—can work well and are easily imported.
- *Video podcast.* A bit more work, especially if you are shooting new scenes, but easy to produce with iMovie. Existing clips can be imported and mixed, titles and narration can be added. iMovie exports directly in standards-based MPEG-4 format that plays on the iPod and most other mobile devices.

Quantity. How long should a podcast be? Long enough to accomplish its purpose, but short enough to work in the podcast setting. The average length of a popular song, on which the iPod experience has been based for most of our students, is 3 to 4 minutes. An episode of *The Daily Show* is about 22 minutes, 15 if you remove the commercials. This is the kind of material iPodders are used to working with. On the other hand, some iPodders listen to talking books over many hours and seem to enjoy the experience.

The length of a podcast should match the context of your students and the nature of your content. How much are they likely to be ready to consume at one sitting? What are the natural chunks that your content divides into? It may work better to design each podcast to teach a single concept or idea rather than an entire lecture or chapter. Students will use your podcasts for review and reference, where shorter episodes make it easier to find what they need to learn and to listen it to it multiple times as necessary. Shorter podcasts are also easier to produce and edit and modify than long ones.

To experience some sample educational podcasts, open iTunes, connect to the iTunes Store, and then click iTunes U in the genre list. Browse some of the featured podcasts. Most of these were homegrown, created by professors and teachers like you. Then search the iTunes U collection for podcasts in your field, using the keyword search feature on that page. You will find examples ranging from 2-minute introductions to 2-hour lecture archives, in all three formats (audio, enhanced, and video). Let these examples inspire your own portable podcast productions.

BUILDING NEVER ENDS

Taking into consideration all of the aspects of Education 3.0: curriculum, grouping and scheduling, teacher development, leadership, and technologies, it's no surprise that in most schools it takes more than a year to build it. And once the first vision is complete, you'll find that the world has changed, and it's time to start the visioning and planning process all over again!

CHAPTER 7

Monitor and Refresh

As you build Education 3.0, you should pay attention to your progress, and let the school community know how you are doing. And once you've completed the construction process, you need to measure how well its results compare with your original vision. Then, when you are sure that Education 3.0 is happening at your school, you should assess the results, using the array of measures outlined in your assessment plan. Finally, after a few years of enjoyment of this new kind of learning, you will be wise to look around and see how the world has changed, and determine whether or not a new educational vision is called for.

TRACK THE TASKS

As you build Education 3.0, you'll use your schedule spreadsheet from Chapter 4 to track your progress. To keep the community involved and supportive of the transformation, consider putting the spreadsheet online, and shading the cells as they are accomplished. You may do this on your school's web site or on Google Docs. To make the tracking easier, let each responsible person on the list shade in the cells they are responsible for as they complete them.

INVENTORY THE IMPLEMENTATION

Even after all the tasks in the action plan are completed, the school may not be fully enmeshed in Education 3.0. Not until all students are enjoying the *Day in the Life* that you envisioned should you be satisfied that your work is complete. So you need a way to monitor the implementation of the vision. This might best be done by repeating the Education 3.0 Inventory that you administered in Step 3 when you scanned the system. Don't do this too soon; make sure the investments and changes have had a chance to work their way down to the classroom level.

As with the scan in Step 3, administer the inventory to both faculty and students, so that you might better understand any differences in perception between the two groups. If your school was practicing Education 2.0 during the first scan, the scores on the inventory would have been quite low; after a year of implementation, you can expect to see a change in this instrument. If you're not seeing a change after 2 years, when you administer this inventory a third time, then something's amiss, and you will want to examine the results closely to understand what's not happening.

ADMINISTER THE ASSESSMENTS

A year after the action plan has been completed, when the implementation has reached through to the classroom level, it's time to administer again the assessments that you used to scan the system in Step 4. Your objective in this process is to see how close the school has come to its vision of Education 3.0. These may include student, faculty, and parent surveys, classroom walk-throughs, and the Faculty Technology Profile. You should also compile other data that measure the effects of your initiatives, such as student attendance and retention rates, scores on standardized exams, graduation rates, and college acceptance rates.

A review of Chapter 4 might be appropriate at this point, especially the section "Assessment of Education 3.0." The discussion there of which types of assessments are likely to show growth and change after the first year is important. Few of your assessments will move from the low end of the scale to the high end in so short a time; the purpose of this midstream monitoring is to identify areas where progress is not being made, so that it might be remedied, and to take note of where things are moving forward, so they might be encouraged.

No matter what you find, the results of the annual assessment of progress should compiled, discussed by the leadership, and made public to the school community, along with the leadership's plan for moving ahead over the next year.

REVISIT THE VISION

After the second or third annual report, when you might expect most aspects of your vision to have come to fruition, you should set up a method to revisit the vision. Is it still adequate to the world that your students will graduate into? Have new technologies opened up new opportunities for better methods of teaching and learning? Have the arts and sciences advanced far enough that we should adjust the curriculum to include the new discoveries?

Scan the workplace. Send a team out to the newest workplaces in your geographic area, the places making new capital investments and offering new jobs. Watch what the workers do. Ask the employers what competencies they look for in their new hires. Take pictures. Bring these back to the leadership team for discussion.

Visit the college. Send a team to the colleges you would like your students to attend. Visit the student union, some classrooms, and the library. Watch how students work and what they work on. Interview some of your own students at this college, and ask them what they wish they had learned in high school to prepare them for what they are doing at college. Take pictures. Bring these ideas back to the leadership team for discussion.

Consider the technology. When you take an airplane trip or ride the commuter train, take note of what devices businesspeople are using to do their work. Visit the leading electronic store in your area and ask which new information technology devices are selling well. Take pictures. Bring these ideas back to the leadership team for discussion.

Review the arts and sciences. Ask your department chairs to review the new developments in their field over the last 3 years, with an eye to which ones might be included in the curriculum. Ask for a recommendation for what might be removed to accommodate the new concepts.

Refresh your vision. Convene the leadership group to consider all that's been gathered by these scans. Determine whether things outside of school have changed enough to warrant the development of a new vision for the school. Should a new vision be needed, go back to Chapter 1 and follow the seven steps as you did before.

Sample *Day in the Life* Stories

The text of Chapter 2, "Set the Vision," includes a description of a day in the life of Sally, a high school student. This appendix supplements Sally's day with those of elementary school student Max, Education 2.5 high school student Justin, high school science teacher Mr. Bacon, and district superintendent Ms Hunter, and also includes a *Moment in the Life* of four college students around the world. All of these Day in the Life stories were compiled from those produced by schools that have gone through the Education 3.0 process.

A DAY IN THE LIFE OF A STUDENT: ELEMENTARY SCHOOL

This Day in the Life story follows an elementary student through a day of schoolwork, to illustrate the key ideas of Education 3.0. Like Sally, our student, Max, starts his day early and takes full advantage of new technologies for learning. Unlike Sally, Max must overcome some severe learning disabilities to succeed in his work. As you follow Max through his day, notice how personal technologies help him overcome his disabilities, and how the nature and scope of his work in elementary school prepare him to for the kind of high school experience you saw with Sally in Chapter 2.

6:30 a.m. Good Morning, Max! His iPod repeats the greeting until Max turns it off. He's waking himself up a half hour early today to video chat with his e-Pal in Scotland while she's still at school.

> Schoolwork starts early for our hypothetical student, as it must if we are to achieve our objectives. The 180 days times 6 hours per day that's allowed in most states is simply not sufficient to develop the skills and talents of youth necessary to succeed in the 21st century. And new communication technologies, such as instant messaging, allow students to be connected with their schoolwork and their colleagues all day, every day.

6:35 a.m. Max checks the temperature outside his window and converts the reading to Celsius on his iPod.

> Our student has learned, from his teachers and friends, how to use a variety of applications on his handheld device. It's part of his tool set for school and he uses it all day long. In this instance, he's getting ready to share temperature data with his e-Pal in Scotland.

6:40 a.m. Max checks the local paper online for sunrise and sunset data for his town. Now, he's ready for his conversation with Kate in which he'll share the week's data.

> Max has learned how to navigate to resources online, how to use applications to analyze data and how to tell stories using data. As more and more information is linked to the Web, school curricula need to be adjusted to take advantage of it and to develop student skill in using it. Despite his severe learning disability that prevents him from decoding words, he is able to participate in this science activity with the help of a mobile device.

6:45 a.m. Max wanders down to the kitchen where his dad is preparing the family breakfast. Max logs onto the family computer in the kitchen and sees Kate online already. He starts up his video chat with Kate, his 10-year-old e-Pal on Sanday, one of the Orkney Islands, exchanging weather and sunrise and sunset data for the week. He finds out that it's only 8 degrees Celsius today on Sanday. Using a spreadsheet program, he adds her data and creates an updated daylight graph which he e-mails to his teacher and to Kate. He notices that Kate's daylight hours are much shorter than they were last week and he records a note on his iPod to ask his teacher about this.

Max tells Kate about the *Abel's Island, Take Two* project and that he's hoping that his group will choose Sanday Island for their project. She asks him to send her the video they'll make. She tells him about an upcoming school trip to Edinburgh and about the seals she saw on the beach earlier that day. She tells him that she got elected to the pupil council at her school.

> The world is much more connected for students at Max's school, E.S. 21+. Students are encouraged to be curious and to ask questions. Max is willing to get up early to make up for the difference in time zones. In fact, Max is willing to do a lot of work before and after school because his projects interest him.

7:00 a.m. Max sends his data and graph to his teacher and to his folder on the school's web server.

> Student work is seldom handed in on paper. Rather, it's kept by each student in online folders and a portfolio, a collection of work that provides evidence of learning to their teachers and their parents.

7:15 a.m. After practicing his noiseless MIDI drums with SmartMusic, he breakfasts with his mom and dad. At breakfast, his mother asks about his upcoming day at school; she knows what's coming up from the teacher's web site and an e-mail reminding her to go over Max's spelling words with him. This week's words are all on a survival theme, connected to the reading of the online *Abel's Island* project.

> Breakfast together and conversations over meals are important in Max's house. Because he has a number of learning challenges, these times are especially important to him. His parents help him process what he's learned, as well as foreshadow what the day will bring. At meals, they often discuss the ideas Max encounters at school. In fact, the school provides on its web site family discussion questions that tie into the curriculum. The family has learned to intervene with Max's learning disability through an online parent training course listed in his IEP.

7:30 a.m. Max uses his iPad to take some pictures of his home, focusing on those items he would most miss if he, like the main character of *Abel's Island,* got stranded on an island. Then he packs his bag for the day: iPad, headphones, lunch, and snack. His bag weighs only about 2 pounds.

> All of Max's text books are online. While there are hard copies available in the classroom, he doesn't carry them back and forth. E.S. 21+ takes advantage of the information devices that students carry in their pockets, adding applications and books online so students are ready for learning at any time in any place.

7:45 a.m. On the bus Max reads a chapter of *Abel's Island* on his iPad, while listening to his teacher read along with him. He stops and repeats, clicks on unknown words, and hears their definition and pronunciation. When he's finished reading, he records his response to the chapter on his iPod. It will be uploaded to the teacher once he reaches school.

In addition to providing the full illustrated textbook for each subject online, the school provides an extensive library of electronic texts that can be downloaded to students' laptops or to their iPads, formatted for ease of reading on these ubiquitous portable devices. Max's teacher knows that Max learns best by listening, but he does need to practice his reading. So the teacher provides podcasts and recorded books to supplement Max's learning in school. These are automatically downloaded as they are needed in the syllabus. When Max clicks a word he doesn't know, his iPad records which words he's selected. These will be available later to his teacher.

8:15 a.m. When Max gets to school, he logs onto the school network from his classroom laptop, registers his attendance and lunch count, uploads his pictures to his folder, greets his teacher, and adds his weather data points to the class chart.

Students themselves carry out many of the day-to-day administrative tasks of the school. Beginning in first grade, before they can read their own names, they learn to click on their picture to register their attendance and lunch preferences. Teachers expect students to contribute to small-group and class projects, carrying out these tasks without being reminded.

8:30 a.m. Max joins his small group in the media center. His group's task today is to brainstorm characters and plot for their upcoming skit on *Abel's Island, Take Two*. The assignment includes shipwrecking them on the shore of an environment very different from their own. Max's group votes to land on Sanday Island, and asks Max lots of questions about it.

Students are used to taking charge of their own projects. They are encouraged to become experts on their own particular slice of a project. Even students with learning challenges can inform the group and extend its learning. The skit they are planning is part of a carefully planned integrated unit, incorporating language arts, geography, science, art, and math skills.

8:45 a.m. The group goes online and spends a few minutes learning about Sanday Island and looking at pictures of Kate's school and some of the migratory birds and seals now in residence. Max uses the online dictionary to read and define words he doesn't know.

Students know how to locate information on the Internet, find a variety of sources and discuss what they are learning—all independently. And they know how to employ mobile technologies to overcome their learning disabilities.

9:00 a.m. Their group advisor (who floats from group to group throughout the period) shows them how to get started planning their project by developing a storyboard with Inspiration software. She quickly shows them how to use Inspiration to map their ideas. They sketch out their skit and send it to their teacher for feedback. One member of the group records voice notes as they go along. They divide up the characters so that each student is responsible for creating a clay character in art class and describing its identity in writing.

> While the teacher is present, the students are used to getting technology instruction on an as-needed, just-in-time basis. They don't visit technology on a weekly basis; they use it daily as needed.

9:45 a.m. The students return to their home-base room for snack and conversation. The teacher asks who were able to reach their e-Pals that day and they share their experiences.

> It's assumed that students will be responsible for doing their homework, which often consists of reaching out beyond the school and community via the Internet. They can do this independently and don't need a special time during the school day to carry out these tasks.

10:00 a.m. Max goes to his small-group math class. Max struggles with math as well as reading. As he settles in for his math lesson, Max plays with NumberLine on his iPad, practicing fractions and decimals.

> The school provides lots of reinforcement for students who struggle, not only small-group instruction, but challenging activities that can be carried in the student's pocket. Max can discreetly play his instructional games and get support at the same time.

10:10 a.m. Max's math teacher uses the daylight graphs from the classroom to develop a lesson on daylight changes over time. He and Max record data from other students' locations: Oahu, St. Maarten, the Aleutian Islands. Together, they notice that the lines are steeper for some locations and shallower for others. The line for the Sanday Island is much steeper than that of St. Maarten. Pulling out a globe, Max's teacher helps him locate the various places. Max is curious about what it all means.

It's not unusual for the math teacher to incorporate geography into his lessons or to use data from the classroom to guide the math lessons he presents. Together, the various teachers make sure to give Max and his peers connected experiences. The visual nature of the graphs allows him to understand the mathematical and geographical concepts despite his reading disability.

11:00 a.m. Max returns to his classroom where a discussion of last night's chapter of *Abel's Island* is underway. He joins in by sharing his images—projected directly from his iPad—of those things he would most miss if he were to get lost on an island away from home.

All students read some shared books and are encouraged to participate in group discussions, whether they do so with images, writing, or speaking. All learning styles are supported.

11:45 a.m. At lunch Max sits with his buddies. They talk about their own projects: While Max's group is using Sanday Island, other groups are using Oahu, the Aleutians, and St. Maarten. They get into a lively debate about why some places have fewer hours of daylight than others. They decide that some places are just lucky. A teacher on duty, overhears the conversation but doesn't provide the answer.

Debate and speculation are encouraged at Max's school. Often, the teachers will respond with a neutral "Hmmm," or ask an extending question, rather than provide quick answers.

12:45 p.m. In his small-group reading class Max plays his podcast reflection of last night's reading homework. He's mastered the difficult passages thanks to the iPad's ability to speak text aloud. Max shares the pictures he took that morning at home. He and his teacher work on a list of accommodations he'd need to make on the island as a way to guide his thinking. Then they work together inventing Max's character for the group skit.

Max gets support from his teachers and parents, but at the same time understands that he needs to figure things out for himself. His teachers firmly believe in the malleability of intelligence, that there are no unintelligent students, but many who may need targeted support as they progress through the school. Max is not discouraged by his learning challenges. He is learning how to meet them with the help of various technologies.

1:15 p.m. In his art class Max constructs a clay figure for the group animation project, after first sketching it on the computer. He has very strong art skills and creates a miniature seal, an exact replica of the seals on Sanday Island.

> Students come with a wide range of skills, and these are encouraged. While Max has serious deficiencies in reading and math, he's able to shine in art class.

2:00 p.m. Max joins his group in the media lab where they combine their ideas and nail down their story. They've each brought a clay figure and one member of the group has produced a background for their claymation. Max comments that it looks remarkably like Hoy Beach on Sanday Island.

2:30 p.m. Working with the video camera on one of their iPads, they set up their movie. Max goes off to ask the music teacher to lend them percussion instruments to get background sounds. Another group member is sent off to find the technology coach (a high school student who is doing this job as his internship) to better understand how they will edit their movie once it's complete. They are eager to use a combination of technologies to tell their story.

> The groups at E.S. 21+ have a strong commitment to each other, each member doing his part. They are not shy about asking for resources and help.

3:00 p.m. Max and his class relax as their teacher reads another chapter from *The Swiss Family Robinson,* relating it to their ongoing study of islands around the world. Finally, they each draw a challenge question out of a basket. Max gets the question, "What island in the world is most densely populated?" To find the answer, Max must determine area and population, then figure out how many people live in each square mile. He grins as he goes out the door: This one's going to be quite a challenge for him!

> Max's school uses every opportunity to relate literature and other topics to provide its students with a rich experience. Daily challenge questions are all related to the topics under study.

3:20 p.m. Max stays for extended day, and logs onto the computer to complete his script. One of his jobs is to spell check and read over the group's document. He finishes this task before joining the after-school games in the gym.

> By giving Max the job of group spell-checker, his teachers and peers build in extra reading practice that has special meaning for his group.

4:30 p.m. At pickup time Max shows his father the clay seal and tells him all about the group's skit. He asks his dad why St. Maarten has a longer day than Sunday. His dad's not sure, but says they can work on that at home.

> The school provides a program of studies that is highly integrated, challenging, and meaningful to its students. Parents enjoy being asked questions they can't immediately answer. They are sure that their children will do well in later years because they are curious, inquisitive, and positive about their learning.

7:00 p.m. After supper, Max goes online with the family computer and is happy to see his group is still online, as is his teacher. They have an impromptu group video conversation about where they'd want to live—in a place with very short winter days or longer ones. Max says he wants to live in a warm place where the days are longer, to which his teacher responds, "Do warm places always have longer days?" Now, it's Max's turn to say "Hmmmm . . . " as he glances over at his dad and mom.

> Learning doesn't stop at 3:20 p.m., and everyone knows it. Rather than spend afternoons and evenings in front of the television, students are encouraged to continue talking to each other, continue debating, and continue learning.

A DAY IN THE LIFE OF A STUDENT: EDUCATION 2.5

The kinds of learning we saw with Sally and Max, and the kinds of teaching that we will see with Mr. Bacon, represent Education 3.0, a far cry from what most schools are doing now. As we learned from Superintendent Hunter in Carson, the process of getting to 3.0 can take several years. And it doesn't happen all at once: students and teachers progress gradually along the path from 2.0 to 3.0.

This *Day in the Life of Justin,* based on the work of school principals in New York City, paints a picture of what Education 2.5 would look like.

Justin is a ninth grader at iZone High School, a hypothetical institution located in a city near you and striving to provide innovative approaches to teaching and learning. Justin is not a model student—far from it. A native Spanish-speaker, he has struggled since kindergarten with the culture of the school and especially learning how to read. And Justin's school is at the early phases of transformation, about halfway from Education 2.0 to 3.0. Let's follow Justin for a day at his new school, where he hopes to move forward toward graduation and success in the world.

As you follow Justin, look for illustrations of the following:

- How time is used differently
- The nature of student responsibility for learning
- The application of technology
- The capabilities of the online curriculum
- The nature of the teacher's role

7:00 a.m. He had set the alarm on his iPod Touch to wake him at this early hour because he was determined to ace the Regents Living Environments practice exam this afternoon. Justin sits up in bed, picks up the iPod, and pulls up the background material on how cells divide, a topic he knows will be on the test. The third word in the sentence stumps him: *mitosis*. He taps it to see a definition. He taps again to hear it. "Mitosis," he repeats to himself. "Sounds like a disease." He taps for more info, and up pops a podcast that shows some little pieces splitting up, followed by the larger object splitting in two. The voice-over explains what's happening. Justin begins to understand what this concept is all about.

> Justin and his school understand that in order to cover all that today's students need to know, the time for academic work needs to extend beyond the 6 hours of the school day. So the school provides every student with a mobile learning device on which the entire curriculum is available, downloaded automatically from the iZone Learning Environment (iLE) whenever Justin is within the reach of the school's Wi-Fi network. Once it's on the iPod, Justin can study at home, on the subway, in school, or wherever he finds himself. And the device is programmed to help him overcome his learning disabilities, with explanations, pronunciations, and podcasts available at the tap of a finger.

8:00 a.m. The science reading starts to make sense now that he understands the basic concept. Like most of the people on the subway this morning, Justin sports white earbuds, but what he listens to is far different—it's the audio version of the Living Environments text. He listens as he reads the words. A quick tap and the iPod switches into Spanish, then back again. When he reaches the end of the section, he gets a quick quiz, drawn from previous years' Regents questions:

> If a chemical that interrupts cell division is added to a culture of human liver tissue, which process would stop?
>
> (1) meiosis
> (2) mitosis
> (3) breakdown of glucose
> (4) diffusion of nutrients

A tap on #2 shows that he has learned something after all. But he's curious, so he taps on answer #1, to learn the difference between mitosis and meiosis. Justin rewards himself for his success by taking some time to sketch a digram of the mitosis process on his iPod Touch.

> With the curriculum in his pocket, Justin can study no matter where he is. Whenever he has a free moment, he gets back to work. His technology provides him the help he needs to overcome his language difficulties, and to help him track his own progress. Audio, video, animation, self-correction, and translation are combined in the online version of the course to enable Justin to learn the key concepts of the subject. And assessment is not a separate and secret activity for Justin: It's built into the online course materials. This reading and practice, which in his old school was done in class during the regular school day, is now accomplished largely outside of school. This enables Justin's teachers to use valuable class time for deeper pursuits of challenging problems.

9:00 a.m. As soon as he enters the school, Justin's attendance is recorded as his iPod comes within range of the wireless network. It's also reflected on the screen of the IP phone on Mr. Marc's desk. In the advisory homeroom Mr. Marc checks the phone display against the faces in front of him and sends a confirming click to the system. He reminds the students to check their personal schedules for the day, to see if anything's been added; some pull out their iPods, some turn to the computers in the classroom. Justin sees his science meeting in red, his math class in green, the play rehearsal in yellow. He adds a personal item in blue at 1:15: "Create mitosis animation." He is interrupted by a plaintive "Do I have to go to this study group today?" from a fellow student. "Why do you suppose they sent you there?" asks Mr. Marc. "Maybe because I scored 56 on the last online quiz in math?" asks the student. No reply is necessary.

> Administrative functions that consumed valuable learning time and expensive paper in Justin's old school take place automatically at iZone High School. In addition, students manage their schedules online, including both school-assigned tasks as well as those they set up for themselves. These calendars are kept on their personal iPods and reflected in the online iZone Learning Environment, where they are available to teachers and parents. The online courses keep track of how students are doing and automatically assign tutorials and tutoring sessions to students who do not seem to be mastering the materials.

9:20 a.m. In the lecture hall Mr. Marc focuses the digital microscope on the cells in the slide, while 75 students watch the action on the Smart-Board. The video output is being webcast through the school's network so that students can watch and record the action in real time on their various mobile devices. "Maria, are you seeing this OK?" asks Mr Marc to a wheelchaired student whose apartment elevator is broken today and so she is studying from home. "When you do this yourselves in the lab," warns Mr. Marc, "pay attention to the temperature of the culture. The cells will die if they get too cold. They're warm now. What do you see happening?" Justin watches the SmartBoard, but he can see more detail on his laptop. "The mass is getting slowly larger," responds Justin. "Now I've got the chemical ready to add. It's one that blocks chromosomal activity. What do you predict will happen?" On Justin's screen appear four choices. He clicks answer #2, "the mass will stay the same size." Looking up to the SmartBoard, he sees that most of the class has chosen answer #3, the mass will shrink. At Mr. Marc's direction, he turns to his neighbor to discuss the reasoning behind their different predictions.

> By doing this science demonstration with 75 students, Mr. Marc effectively frees up two other teachers to do joint planning or tutor students who need extra help or prepare a special demonstration of their own. By using a digital microscope, he can allow all students to see what's happening, even those at home, and record the results for later analysis. By asking students to observe and predict, he is modeling the scientific method. By collecting their predictions online and reflecting them back immediately, he is fomenting thinking and discussion. By letting the online course do most of the basic presentation of concepts, Mr. Marc is freed up to develop and

conduct demonstrations and labs that go deeper into the topic and inspire students to apply what they've learned online to a real-world problem.

10:00 a.m. It's Justin's assigned work time, so he finds a comfortable spot in the school to pursue his online coursework. He chooses the library, finds a chair and a table, and connects to the iZone Learning Environment. The iLE suggests that he'd profit from some work on his algebra course this morning, so he clicks into it on the laptop he checked out earlier in the day. The first assignment in Section 5 of the course is a word problem: If a single cell divides in half once each day, how long will it take to increase to a million cells? Justin knows he needs to use x's and y's to find the answer, but he doesn't know where to start. So he consults the online coach that's built into the system. "Write down what you know, "suggests the coach. Justin enters 1,000,000, which is the number of cells he wants to get to. "Now put that into the form of an equation." So Justin puts an equal sign in front of it. And so forth until the problem is solved.

Each student at the iZone School is scheduled for work time each day, when they pursue their online course content. The school has set up spaces conducive to this kind of work. And the online courses are more than simply electronic copies of the old textbook: They include well-designed problems, multimedia tutorials, and online help. While Justin is working independently on math, his math teacher may be teaching a face-to-face class, tutoring a small group of students, or doing curriculum development with other teachers.

11:00 a.m. In his global history class period Justin works with four other students around a table to design a response to the plague. They are role-playing the leadership council of a European city in AD 1325. Justin's task was to find out how much if anything doctors knew of germ theory during that time, so that their group's plan would be historically accurate. He had done his research online, during yesterday's work time at school and last night at home on his iPod. He projected onto the SmartBoard from his iPod a drawing from a 14th-century manuscript that he'd found online, that seemed to show plague germs as expanding cell masses. He could not read the Latin captions, so he wasn't sure what exactly it was. Another student in his group showed him how to translate the Latin on his laptop, and they all learned that Justin's illustration was in fact depicting the expansion of bubbles in rising bread.

Teachers at Justin's school work together to plan a curriculum that is coordinated from one subject to another and uses a variety of student groupings and teaching methods. They also go out of their way to ensure that these methods take full advantage of online resources and local technologies. At least once each day, each student works in a collaborative group with a highly structured long-term assignment. This helps them develop the problem-solving and social skills needed for success in the 21st-century college and workplace environments. Justin's day consists of a careful balance of large-group, small-group, and individual work, carried out online and in person.

12:00 Noon. Justin is way ahead of the rest of his elective art class in basic drawing. He asks his teacher—who's actually a designer at a studio downtown with whom Justin is doing his credit-bearing field work—if he can use today's class time to develop an animation of mitosis. They meet together over video conference every other day. He shows her the sketch he developed earlier in the day. He thinks he can design something that will help other students better understand the key concepts of mitosis. Permission granted, he transfers the sketch he drew earlier from his iPod to the school's multimedia workstation, fires up Photoshop, and goes to work. After consulting the online medical illustration library at the nearby university, as well as the explanations from a half-dozen online texts and recent Regents exam questions on this topic, his animation faithfully represents the process in just the amount of detail that a student would need to succeed on the test. Justin saves the animation to his portfolio on the school server.

Each student at iZone High School takes an elective course that in most cases includes field work and a mentor from the world outside of school. Most of these mentors handle a small group of students. They maintain contact over the network, communicating regularly through video, audio, and images. Justin will get school credit from his animation project, which will be critically evaluated by his science teacher and his art mentor as soon as it's complete and in his online portfolio. And the technology tools that Justin uses to create this work are the same ones used in the real world.

1:00 p.m. English Language Arts has long been Justin's downfall. He's the first in his family to learn this language, and his test scores have always hovered near the bottom. But this year, it's not so bad. They're reading Martin Luther King's "I Have a Dream" speech. He's got a copy on his iPod, a print copy, and a podcast version of the film taken at the event itself. Today's lesson is about metaphors; Justin taps the word on his iPod to learn its meaning, but this is not enough; he asks the teacher to give some examples. On the SmartBoard she shows a section of the speech as Justin watches and listens, "and righteousness flows like a mighty stream." A discussion ensues: what's *righteousness*? Does it flow like water? Can you find another metaphor in the speech? Justin scrolls through the text on his iPod. The student next to him has found an online analysis of the speech. They work together on the sentence, "I have a dream that one day even the state of Mississippi, a desert state, sweltering with the heat of injustice and oppression, will be transformed into an oasis of freedom and justice." Despite the many words that aren't in his reading vocabulary, Justin with the help of his iPod begins to understand this idea of metaphor.

> The online curriculum is brought to bear in regular teacher-led classes as well as for independent study at the iZone High School. So are the mobile technologies that help students overcome their disabilities. Through the iZone Learning Environment, teachers have access to video libraries, analytical works, and teaching ideas all keyed to the state standards and to the books they are reading. Justin's teachers have learned to incorporate the classroom technologies and mobile devices and online course materials into everyday teaching and learning in such a way that class sessions are more interesting and go deeper into the core ideas of the curriculum. Even though the students receive much of their instruction online, the teacher maintains a key role in learning.

2:00 p.m. Justin huddles with his study group just before the practice exam. They share sample test questions and key ideas. They take the test online, some from the library's laptops, some from their iPods. The results from the multiple-choice section come back right away: Justin got 8 of the 10 questions correct, second-best in his group. They'll get the essay portion returns tomorrow. On his way out the door, headed for his internship downtown, Mr. Marc asks Justin if he might submit his mitosis animation to the iLE Living Environments course as a candidate for inclusion in the online curriculum. "I saw it as I was reviewing your online portfolio. Nice work."

> The online curriculum is not fixed in stone; teachers can modify and update it easily for their own students, and submit improved examples and lessons to a committee of peers who can add them to the official course. In this way the science teachers have formed a community of practitioners who are constantly improving the quality of the coursework—sometimes with the help of their students.

A DAY IN THE LIFE OF A TEACHER

What does Education 3.0 look like through the eyes of a teacher? Next to the student, the teacher is the most important player on this new stage. What happens to the student in the course of a day is determined in large measure by the teacher's work. So we'll continue our journey toward Education 3.0 by following Mr. Bacon, Sally's science teacher, through a day of work at his school, H.S. 21+.

7:00 a.m. The alarm on Mr. Bacon's iPhone chimes to wake him and remind him of his tasks for the day: to check in with the students in his project group, to install a real-time water-quality monitoring station, and to participate in the districtwide science curriculum meeting—all in addition to his teaching duties. Another busy day!

> Mr. Bacon's day is varied, with several hours scheduled to lead lectures and labs, but time set aside for guiding a project group and setting up research experiments. At H.S. 21+ students spend a third of their day on independent work, not under the direct supervision of a teacher,which frees Mr. Bacon and his colleagues for other tasks.

7:10 a.m. Mr. Bacon sits down at his laptop for his morning routine. His project group's wiki shows some early morning activity: Sally, one of his students, has posted a graph showing alarming levels of PCB contamination in the city's drinking water. Noticing that Sally's conclusions were based on very few data points, Mr. Bacon posts a suggestion that she resample the data later in the day.

7:12 a.m. Continuing his morning checks, he calls up the activity logs from his online environmental chemistry course. Next to the names of the 17 students—from all over the district—he sees what they have been working on over the last 24 hours. He notices that despite completing the quiz on pH levels at 2:00 a.m., Fred in Flushing earned a perfect score, and sends him a quick congratulatory note. He denies (politely and patiently) Alicia's request for another extension on her research proposal.

> Frequent contact with students is even more important in the digital age. Whether they're enrolled in his online course or working in his project group, Mr. Bacon knows that daily monitoring and feedback, with a human touch, is the key to learning—and an interesting way to practice his professional craft.

8:00 a.m. Mr. Bacon meets his project group and a city highway supervisor at the Darwin Street bridge. Together they install and test a solar-powered, real-time data probe with wireless network connection that measures water temperature, pH, and other variables. The students have been planning this installation for the past 2 months, and it goes smoothly. They met especially early in order to do the work at low tide.

> Teachers at H.S. 21+ are encouraged to design and conduct field-based research projects with their students, to focus them on issues of community concern, and to take advantage of the latest digital technologies. From these projects students learn not only their science and math, but also the politics of working with public agencies and the practicalities of real-world installations.

8:30 a.m. *Tick* goes Mr. Bacon's iPhone as he marks Alicia absent from his chemistry class. Almost immediately a message pops back that Alicia is excused today to work with her project group at the art museum. Zach's absent mark, however, goes into the system and is automatically communicated to his parent's mobile phone through a text message.

8:32 a.m. He also sees on his phone eleven warnings that students under his care had wandered off campus. These were sent by the GPS-equipped iPods that all students carry. Mr. Bacon is concerned, until he reads the list, sees the names of his project group students, the pins on the map concentrated on the Darwin Street bridge, and the time stamp at 8:35 a.m.

> H.S. 21+ takes full advantage of digital communication tools to manage information about the students they are responsible for. This not only reduces paperwork and clerical expense, it also provides a measure of security that enables students to be given more freedom in their work places.

9:30 a.m. Mr. Bacon participates in the districtwide chemistry curriculum development meeting from his classroom at H.S. 21+. The meeting is conducted through WebEx; Mr. Bacon has focused his iPad on the new lab sensor he has been testing, so the other teachers at the meeting can see the probe as the data displays in a real-time graph in the WebEx window, and hear Bacon's commentary.

> Teachers from all over the district collaborate regularly on curriculum and professional development, without leaving their classrooms.

Thy use the same mobile and desktop video conferencing tools that are employed in business, that enable the full range of human communication methods: voice, video, whiteboard, image, and text.

10:30 a.m. In an instant message conversation with student Fred from Flushing, Mr. Bacon discusses the quality of the online tutorials that both of them have been reviewing. He needs an efficient way for all students to learn how to use the new data probes that he's just installed in the lab. They agree that students will learn the most from the podcast tutorials developed by the science education faculty at Hunter College and published as iBooks by McGraw-Hill. He checks that the district has licensed these tutorials—which make extensive use of digital video—and then links them to his class page on the school's learning management system.

Teachers at H.S. 21+ don't waste class time teaching skills that are best learned independently online by students. Nor do they need to develop all of their own curriculum materials. Instead, they take advantage of the academic and publishing community that more and more shares its new developments online, creating tutorials that can be played on mobile devices as well as computers. And the teachers at H.S. 21+ often involve their students in selecting the best of them.

11:30 a.m. With a half hour to spare before his next class, Mr. Bacon works on an assignment in the online course that he is taking to help him integrate the new environmental lab probes into the Regents chemistry course. After working his way through the video-on-demand segments of the course, he completes this last assignment. Once his work is checked by the online instructor, he'll send his record to the district superintendent to get professional development credit for this work.

Like his students, Mr. Bacon is always learning new things, often through focused online professional development tutorials that are linked closely to what he is doing in class. He can learn whenever and wherever he has the opportunity—in school, at home, even at the beach—since most courses are delivered in formats that can be deployed on handheld mobile devices.

12:03 p.m. With the experiment set to run on the demo table, Mr. Bacon polls the large lecture class. "How many of you predict that the data will appear as in the first result table?" No hands go up; instead a graph grows in real time on the big screen as the students' responses are tallied and displayed—they entered their predictions on their iPods, which linked to Bacon's computer through the school's wireless network, and where interactive software compiles the results into a real-time graph. "Looks like 43 of you predict the first result, 54 the second, and the rest of you the third. The class is about equally divided on what's going to happen, so we'll need to discuss this some more before I run the experiment."

> Teachers at H.S. 21+ sometimes work with very large classes, especially when demonstrating dramatic sequences or delivering special performances suitable to large groups. While Mr. Bacon is teaching 150 in the auditorium, his colleagues are free to engage in research and in small-group work with other students. The plenary sessions often take advantage of digital technologies to make these sessions interactive and thought-provoking.

1:30 p.m. Mr. Bacon listens to his project group as they prepare for their upcoming presentation. He suggests they gather one more round of data, with a larger sample, before publishing their conclusions about PCB levels in the river. He also shows them how to use a spreadsheet to fit a mathematical curve to the data points they have collected from their water samples.

> Each teacher at H.S. 21+ is assigned a project group: 6–12 students who design and carry out an action research project in the community. Both teacher and students get as much credit for this course as they do for any other. It has become the opportunity for many interesting educational practices . . .

1:40 p.m. He relates the resulting sine function to sound waves; this spurs a discussion of music, into which the students inject (from their humanities class of the previous period) ideas of the Romantic era, reflected in lush pastoral themes in both music and art. As they discuss, Mr. Bacon finds in the school's digital media library online a painting from the Hudson River School that depicts the (old) Darwin Street bridge. Meanwhile a student locates and plays a Brahms composition retrieved form the same library. The multimedia juxtaposition provides an interesting moment of reflection for all.

> . . . including applications of technology to interdisciplinary linkages. The school's extensive array of fully indexed online resources makes this kind of connection possible. Mr. Bacon enjoys this kind of teaching.

1:55 p.m. His project group is interrupted by an instant message from the district superintendent that arrives on Mr. Bacon's iPod. "Just got a call from the chairman of the school board. He says someone from the school is monitoring the pollution from the General Selectric factory just up the river, and he wants to know why. You have anything to do with this? (Our current board chair is the COO of that plant.)"

1:56 p.m. Mr. Bacon puts the IM up on the big screen for the class to see. "What should we do about this?" he asks them. They suggest offering to deliver their presentation at the factory to its management group. Bacon responds accordingly to the superintendent, who likes the idea. The students assign one of their group to compose a letter for the superintendent to send to the factory operator.

> Teachers at H.S. 21+ are expected to interact with the community and involve students in careful and critical study thereof. The faculty has learned to do this in a way that melds the newest technologies with old-fashioned political sensitivity. Even the superintendent uses IM.

2:30 p.m. As he leaves the project group meeting room, Mr. Bacon notices a graph on one of the school's digital signage boards. It shows the results of the just-released online survey of H.S. 21+ students and parents. Four-to-one they prefer digital curriculum materials to paper textbooks; six-to-one they favor the addition of community service to the school's graduation requirements. And at the bottom of the board he sees a reminder of tomorrow's faculty-student charity basketball match.

> You don't hear bells or loudspeaker announcements at H.S. 21+; instead, public communication takes place through the digital network, directed to relevant individuals, groups, or the school community at large as appropriate, and taking advantage of a variety of reception devices, from iPhones to IP telephones to iPads to digital signage in the hallways.

3:30 p.m. Mr. Bacon practices his two-hand set shot in the gymnasium, in preparation for tomorrow's charity match. On a break, he uses his iPod to check the readings from the probe that his students put onto the Darwin Street bridge in the morning. No data—the graph is flat-lined. He sends an IM to Alicia, his student whose internship is located just across the street from the bridge, and who arranged to use her company's wireless connection to link the data probe to the network. She asks her supervisor to reset the router, and the data flow freely once more.

The network is always with Mr. Bacon, and like the other teachers at H.S. 21+, he uses it all day, from wherever he works or plays, to check on the progress of his projects and his students. Many educational devices connect to the network for the people of H.S. 21+, from iPods to mobile phones, from laptops to data probes, from IP telephones to digital signage. This robust and open network is the key to their educational creativity and flexibility—and keeps students connected with the school even while they are working their internships.

8:00 p.m. The calendar alarms on Mr. Bacon's mobile phone and laptop go off simultaneously in his home office. Time for the WebEx call with his science-teacher colleague in Japan, where it's early morning. As they discuss how they are using the new probes in their teaching, Mr. Bacon sees that his project group has posted the first draft of their podcast presentation to their wiki. He links the podcast to his Japanese colleague, who plans to show it to his students as soon as they arrive.

The digital network knows few national boundaries. And 21st-century teaching crosses many cultures. Teachers at H.S. 21+ are encouraged to involve their students in studies that circle the globe.

10:00 p.m. Snoozing in his study, Mr. Bacon is awakened by Mrs. Bacon, who suggests he tune his laptop to the 10 o'clock news. He follows her advice just in time to see his project group's podcast playing in the background in a meeting room at the state senate. "The anti-pollution bill passed the committee on a 6–4 vote this evening," reports the commentator. "The crucial compromise on the allowable levels of PCB's in water supplies was catalyzed by a podcast prepared by students at H.S. 21+ in Carson City . . . " With a smile, Mr. Bacon puts all of his digital devices, as well as himself, to sleep.

A DAY IN THE LIFE OF A SUPERINTENDENT

What does Education 3.0 look like through the eyes of the superintendent? This Day in the Life story is about a school leader in Carson Unified, the school district that houses H.S. 21+, where Sally and Mr. Bacon spend their days. It follows Ms. Hunter through a day of work to illustrate the educational ideas that form the core of Education 3.0.

4:45 a.m. The alarm on Ms. Hunter's mobile phone chimes with a flashing icon of falling snow. This means it's snowing at more than one

inch per hour at the online weather station at H.S. 21+. The students pro-
grammed it to send an automatic message when the sensor reached this
threshold level. She wakes her laptop, checks in with the SuperWeath-
erWiki (set up by a student project group at the high school) where her
local colleagues coordinate school closings. No one else is closing today.
She links to the local radar weather map and sees a weak front moving
through. An instant message arrives from the bus supervisor, reminding
her of the new snow tires on all the district vehicles. She calls up the online
security camera at the back door of the middle school and sees snow melt-
ing as fast as it falls. Lights off, back to sleep.

> This education leader is not afraid of the nitty gritty of school
> operations, in part because she has harnessed the power of digital
> tools and networks to make her work more efficient. And the
> camera at the middle school, though designed as part of the safe-
> and-secure technology package, turns out to be useful for other
> purposes as well.

8:00 a.m. At the office Ms. Hunter connects the microphone to her
laptop and records *This Week at Carson,* her weekly podcast on the state of
education in the district. Her assistant adds images to the recording, and
sends it to the district's online Digital Media System, which adds it to the
public web site. Community members who subscribe to the podcast will
find it automatically downloaded to their computers and iPods.

> Online multimedia enable the leadership to communicate with
> the public; the same servers and networks provide a wealth of
> on-demand instructional videos and podcasts for students and
> teachers. Standards-based video formats and a robust network
> enable the same digital resource to be displayed on everything from
> the 20-foot screen in the auditorium at H.S. 21+ to the iPod in the
> pocket of a sixth grader.

9:30 a.m. Her online calendar reminds Ms. Hunter of a WebEx meeting with the chemistry curriculum committee. On her laptop she watches
a teacher demonstrate with live video a new laboratory technology they
plan to use, and ask her opinion on how well it matches with the 21st-
century skill set that the district has just adopted. Ms. Hunter replies posi-
tively, and shows a link to a new video clip from the ASCD (Association
for Supervision and Curriculum Development, a national professional
organization) that explains the importance of real-time data analysis to
student learning. The clip downloaded to the district's Digital Media System as part of a subscription with the national curriculum organization.

Desktop video conferencing technology enables full-fledged
participation in policy meetings by all constituents no matter where
they are working. Everyone in the district aims their professional and
curriculum development work at a common set of new skills that will
be essential to their students' future. And digital video on demand
through the network provides a rich set of resources for learning by
both educators and students.

10:00 a.m. At an elementary school n downtown Carson City, Hunter
conducts a *walk-through*—an unannounced visit with the principal to three
classrooms. She does this in a different school each week, not to evaluate
the teachers, but to ascertain the presence of 21st-century skills in this elementary school. She takes notes on her iPod about what she sees, and captures a video clip of an especially provocative discussion among a small
group of students. Later in the week her notes and the video clip will be
the subject of a faculty meeting at the school.

21st-century skills, and the many different ways they can be
developed, are on everyone's mind in Carson Unified, and the focus
is on what happens in the classroom. The leaders at the building
and district level spend many hours each week in classrooms,
looking for evidence of the kind of teaching and learning that lead
to these skills.

10:45 a.m. Back in her office Ms. Hunter turned her attention to candidates for a teaching position in the district. The video clip in the online
portfolio showed excellent elocution and powerful presentation skills on
the part of the first candidate, but little student engagement, and no evidence of 21st-century skill development. The second candidate sent up
by the hiring committee was not nearly as polished, but her video clip
showed an ability to pose questions, listen to students' responses, and
delve deeper into their thinking. Hunter checks out her responses to the
Teacher Technology Profile, adds her impressions to the running commentary from the rest of the committee, and then schedules a live WebEx
interview—the candidate works in another district 250 miles away—for
tomorrow.

School leaders at Carson Unified know more than ever before about
the teachers they hire, with online portfolios, video evidence of
teaching practice, and the ability to interview over the network.
The digitization of the candidate's record makes it easier for more
people to be involved in the hiring process.

11:30 a.m. After checking his online personalized professional development plan, Ms. Hunter approves three credits for science teacher F. Bacon at H.S. 21+, who has completed an online course in deploying probeware in high school science courses. She recalls a photo of Bacon and his students, smiling in muddy boots and mosquito nets, that appeared in the local paper under the headline "Environmental Activists."

Each teacher in the district develops with the principal a personal professional development plan for the year, always aimed at 21st-century skills, and stored online. More and more, their plans include distance-learning exercises focused on new methods for teaching their subject specialty.

1:30 p.m. A new window pops up in Hunter's instant messenger. It's from a neighbor who works at the General Selectric plant just up the river. He is concerned that student activists from H.S. 21+ are preparing to release unpleasant information about his company. A quick IM exchange calms down the insistent industrialist, and reveals that a group of high-school-age students were seen placing some kind of pollution-measuring device on a bridge downstream from the plant. Nothing more. Hunter agrees to find out what's up, pings Bacon by IM, and reports back to the neighbor, all within 2 minutes.

The people who conduct the business of Carson Unified schools, from the board to the leaders, to the teachers, to the parents, to the students, use a wide variety of digital communication channels to work with each other, the most useful of them being instant messaging: less interrupting than a phone call, faster than an e-mail, more efficient than voice, and easier for the receiver to manage.

2:30 p.m. To prepare for her meeting with the state education department later in the afternoon, Hunter analyzes attendance data from the high school over the last 5 years, which is now stored on the school attendance server for easy access. Her analysis shows that the attendance rate has risen by four points over the last 2 years, since the server began sending automatic messages—by e-mail, IM, text, or voice as the parents desire—whenever their children are absent.

Attendance is not just an administrative detail in Carson Unified; it's a key indicator of students' engagement with school, and as such deserves the attention of the leadership. The application of technology to this issue has made it easier to manage, from the reporting through the teachers' IP phones to the parent messaging, to the analytical reports.

4:30 p.m. From the telepresence room down the hall near the mayor's office, Hunter explains to the State Deputy Education Commissioner across the virtual table from her how the parent messaging system at Carson works and how it has helped raise the attendance rate. A school leader from another part of the state asks her about parent reaction to this seemingly obtrusive system. The discussion is fast, furious, personal, and productive.

Hunter travels less and less to the state capital for meetings, yet finds herself more involved with her peers and with statewide educational issues. High-quality video conferencing lets key leaders meet as the need arises, without the time and expense of travel, yet permits honest and frank discussion of sensitive issues with the full gamut of human expression.

7:30 p.m. At the school board meeting, Hunter displays from her iPad the slide comparing the future cost of printed textbooks versus online courseware. She juxtaposes this graph on the big screen with the results of the recent survey of students, parents, and teachers on the same issue. The discussion ranges far and wide, until a majority of the board votes to shift the district's policy toward digital materials wherever possible.

The data and presentations the school leader needs are accessible through the network, on a computer, or on a mobile device: same digital format, same display. The systems and the devices are designed to work together following open standards that are compatible with a wide range of platforms. And data are used throughout the system for decision making at all levels, from the students conducting their research at H.S. 21+ to the citizen representatives in the board room.

10:00 p.m. Watching the nightly local news, Hunter hears of the H.S. 21+ students' podcast at the state legislature. She sends a quick message through the district's learning management system to the students in that project group, congratulating them and their teacher on the quality and effect of their work. A carbon copy (cc) goes to each student's digital portfolio. As she falls asleep, she wonders if any of those students know what a carbon copy really is.

H.S. 21+'s learning management system knows which students are in the various groups and courses, and makes it easy for their teachers and leadership to target a message to a particular group. It's not unusual for the district leadership to involve themselves with the work of students, and the technology makes it possible to do so.

A MOMENT IN THE LIFE:
HIGHER EDUCATION IN A GLOBAL CONTEXT

This book is based mostly in work with K–12 schools building Education 3.0. But many colleges and universities are moving along the same path. This *Moment in the Life* draws from their visions of education, with a special emphasis on global cooperation. This section looks through the eyes of some students and teachers at this new style of higher education. It's just a glimpse, a moment in time in Education 3.0, in several venues.

6:00 a.m. Rolling River, USA. Nineteen point four volts. And that's at the peak height of the sun for today at the test installation in France. Not quite high enough. Each day before breakfast Charlotte checks the output of the photoelectric fabric, so she can take it to her 8 a.m. physics course at Rolling River State College (RRSC) and combine it with the readings of the other sites monitored by fellow undergraduates. She IMs her French colleague Philippe at his internship at DJT/France (Dian Jua Tissu company, international manufacturer of photoelectric fabric) to find out how brightly the sun is shining. "Brouillé" is the reply. Charlotte passes this unknown word to the translator on her laptop and immediately understands the low reading. There's fog in the air over there. Just then she gets another IM from Kofi, in Africa.

> In Education 3.0, higher education is global, practical, and thoughtful. And carried out in large measure online. It's not centered on a classroom or a college, but on the student and the problem to be solved. Learning is not individual and competitive, but social and collaborative. It strives not to produce better test scores but to create new knowledge and apply it to important issues. We see this manifested in Charlotte's international applied research project and her easy use of networked digital technologies.

12:00 noon Kinshasa, Africa. Kofi sends an instant message to fellow student Charlotte: "Can you help me with these physics equations?"

He has been struggling with the equation $E = I*R$. He's not used to representing quantities with letters, and at age 32 it's not easy to learn new approaches, even when they arrive online as part of his degree program at the Mandela Community College, which has partnered with RRSC. Charlotte suggests that Kofi call up a video animation of the relationship between current, voltage, and resistance during his lunch break at the DJT Mine. The tungsten he helps extract from the earth goes to China to be manufactured into the new photoelectric fabric invented at DJT in France and based on physics research done at RRSC. But not for long; as soon as the DJT factory in Kinshasa is complete, Kofi and his fellow Africans will be ready to operate it, and they'll be manufacturing the fabric right here. After mastering his equations, Kofi checks on the loading of the freighter that's bound for China with another load of metal.

> For the developing world, the additional university seats that they desperately need are seldom found in college buildings, but often located in workplaces and homes. Without the luxury of sending midcareer workers to the 4-year adult sleep-over camp that typifies the traditional American and European college, these rising nations harness the Internet, foreign expertise, and the energy of their young populations to learn while they work. Closely entwined with the global economic forces that have changed the face of the workplace, the new higher education system provides just-in-time learning to the most people at the lowest cost. Retraining of midcareer workers, and degree-completion for those who veered off the academic track, is an important mission for higher education systems in all economies. The power of the human network lets these varied types of students learn together, all over the world.

6:00 p.m. Guangzhou, China. The money to fuel the freighter has been wired to Africa, the local factory workers have been paid for the week, and the front doors of the bank have closed for the day. Bank manager Yuan Lao connects to his WebEx session with Grant Grayson III in Rolling River. Grant is studying Chinese online at the South China University of Technology, so Lao greets him with a hearty "Ni hao!" Grant runs his family's bank in Rolling River and has been meeting weekly with his counterpart in Guangzhou in a joint learning expedition that will help both of them better understand the banking laws and traditions of their respective countries. Lao's bank is financing the new solar fabric factory in Africa, while Grayson's manages the American investment in the joint-venture factory in China—both with significant capital from Society DJT in Bayeux, France.

Learning continues long after schooling is complete. Mature adults in high positions are not afraid of taking on the role of student— or of teacher. The world changes in one's lifetime, and all must educate themselves in order to adapt to it, sometimes in a formal school setting, sometimes informally with peers and mentors. New networked technologies make this possible, and online social networks enable a wide choice of media and methods. The new forms of learning combine the disciplines of language, culture, law, and science to tackle the tasks of the day in ways that would rankle the faculty assemblies on many traditional college campuses. Instead of selfishly defending their turf, universities in Education 3.0 collaborate with each other and with industry to take advantage of each other's expertise.

12:00 noon Bayeux, France. Weaving had for centuries been a part of the culture in Bayeux. The photoelectric fabric developed in the lab 2 years ago evolved from a long local tradition of laying warp and weft to create textiles for clothing, industry, art, and the navy. The DRRT (Directeur Regional de la Recherche et la Technologie, a higher education official jointly funded by the university, business interests, and the government) would visit this afternoon to check on the progress of the latest research project, funded jointly by the French government and Societé DJT, to increase the output of the solar cloth. Philippe, a student at the local IUT (Institut Unversitaire Technologique, a 2-year postsecondary technical school closely aligned with local industry), stretches the test samples across their cradles and monitors the digital instruments, all of which are networked over IP to fellow students in the USA and Africa. "Too bad about the fog," muses Philippe. "We'll point the webcast camera out the window so the off-campus students can see for themselves. And connect the light meter directly to the network so they can download the data immediately."

In Education 3.0, higher education is not defined by institution or discipline. And the line between learning, research, and practical problem solving is purposely blurred. Governments, companies, and individuals all invest in learning and research; none has a monopoly; all contribute to moving the society to a new level of economic development and intellectual understanding. Some of the most valuable people in the learning society are those who can see through the fog of tradition, technology, and possibility and pull together diverse groups into new learning clusters.

6:01 a.m. USA. Charlotte downloads the data file from France as soon as it's posted. Today, there's a note attached from the research project director: "I've included both the electrical output data and the light-meter readings from the last week. As you can see, the results do not track as I thought they would: the correlation is far from perfect. I need all of your brains working together to figure out why." Charlotte plots the data on her iPad. It's closely aligned, but there are days when the lines diverge, the sunshine rising while the voltage lags about an hour behind.

12:01 p.m. Africa. Kofi downloads the data from France as it arrives. $E = I*R$ was easy compared with this. All these data to analyze! Kofi invites his colleague Charlotte in the USA, who's in his online physics course, to a WebEx session. (High-school students in the local Network Academy course have recently redesigned the network at DJT so it can handle video as well as data, enabling Kofi to participate fully in the session.) He shares his spreadsheet on the screen, asking her to remind him how to plot the data on his laptop. Kofi sees the same anomaly in the graph. "It seems always to happen in the morning," he notices, "but not every morning. What's going on?"

6:01 p.m. China. Yuan Xiao, the banker's son, plots the same data on his desktop workstation. The sun set a half hour ago, so it's time to go home. As he leaves the DJT factory where he works, he runs his hand across a roll of photoelectric fabric in the yard. It's wet. He wipes his hand on his coat and goes back to his computer to send a note to his fellow students in the physics course. He joins the WebEx session that's in progress. He asks, "In English, what do you call the little droplets of water that grow on the grass in the early morning or at sunset?"

6:02 a.m. USA. "Dew, "replies Charlotte.

12:02 p.m. Africa. "I thought it was called fog," writes Kofi.

12:02 p.m. France. "Brouillé, that's what it is," writes Philippe. "When the fog comes in, the fabric gets wet."

12:03 p.m. Africa. "And even when the sun comes back out, the moisture remains until it's burned off," remarks Kofi.

6:03 a.m. USA. "And when the stuff is wet, it does not produce as much voltage," concludes Charlotte. Smiles all around. Charlotte, who's preparing to teach science in high school, writes up this problem-solving case study, and posts it to the learning management system at the school where she's doing her student teaching.

> Problem solving is a key skill for the new economy, and so it's central to the higher education curriculum—and to the high-school course of study—in the learning society. In this example, the research director presents to his students a problem to which he does not know the answer, a problem that will require them to apply what they have learned in a new way—and to collaborate across continents as they do so. This is an example of the kinds of nonroutine cognitive-analytic task that is becoming more important in the workplace and the laboratory. The students in this example are doing all of the following:
>
> - Gathering, synthesizing, and analyzing information from real-world events
> - Working autonomously with minimal supervision
> - Leading others though their knowledge and influence
> - Thinking critically and asking the right questions
> - Communicating effectively using technology
>
> These are the new skills that the learning society is designed to develop in all its members. And as they learn, these students are :
> - Active and social
> - Motivated to figure things out for themselves so they can advance
> - Bringing different types of knowledge to bear on the group problem
> - Starting from very different places economically and educationally
> - Integrating their learning into their work, and vice-versa

That's a quick glimpse, a moment in Education 3.0 at the college level. It illustrates new possibilities for education at the university level, new approaches to what we need to learn, how we learn it, and who's in charge. The technologies to build this kind of system exist today; our task is to harness them to serve the needs of the Charlottes, Kofis, Philippes, Grants, Laos, and Xiaos of the world. And in turn the needs of their societies.

Case Studies in Education 3.0

These four case studies describe Education 3.0 in four different ways in four very different communties. The NYC iSchool tells the story of an urban high school built on a new approach to teaching and learning. The Watershed descibes a problem-baased curriculum unit that turns the pyramid of study upside down and unifies work across disciplines in a rural school district in Connecticut. The case studies from Mesa, Arizona and Tech Park in upper New York State show two different approaches to creating an educational vision.

THE NYC iSCHOOL

There's a public high school in New York City that's unlike any school you've ever seen. Teaching and learning at this school happen in ways that make perfect sense but do not follow the typical traditions of the American high school. And the role of technology is even more interesting. The author of this book has learned in, taught in, and visited hundreds of high schools in the United States and around the world. They harbor surprising similarities. With few exceptions, they organize themselves according to the 25/C/1/1/1/6 plan:

- 25 students of the same age are grouped together, in a
- Classroom of about 900-square feet, with
- 1 teacher, learning
- 1 subject, for about
- 1 hour, and they repeat this about
- 6 times per day.

And the technologies of learning under this popular plan focus on the printed book and the chalkboard; seldom do networked digital technologies invade these rooms or the teaching that goes on in them. Likewise, the furniture is the same: 25 tablet chairs, a bookcase or two, and a teacher's desk.

Compare this environment and this style of working with what goes on in the world of work in the information economy, or in the modern university. Everything's different in the real world: there's little age segregation; seldom do 25 people work together as a group in a large undivided space; seldom is one person in charge up front; seldom do people restrict themselves to one discipline for a full hour; and seldom does the day repeat itself hour by hour.

And yet it's hard to find high schools that don't follow this ubiquitous 25/C/1/1/1/6 plan—unless you're at the corner of Broome Street and Sixth Avenue in New York City. On the fifth floor of the old Chelsea High School you'll find a group of educators and students who follow a very different model. Their unique way of working is based on some guiding questions posed by the school's coleaders, Alisa Berger and Mary Moss:

- How do we best prepare students for the new world they are graduating into?
- What do they need to be successful in the world of college and work that has changed so much in the last few years?
- What should we really be teaching? How? When? Where?
- How do we at the same time prepare them for the state exams that they must pass to graduate?
- How can technology best contribute to learning what they need?

The answers to these questions led them to a very different model of organization, time, teaching, and technology. The learning approach at the iSchool centers on five components:

- Short-term, intensive interdisciplinary challenge modules, based on real-world problems. The problems become the curriculum, developing subject matter concepts as well as 21st-century skills, and getting students involved in the world outside the walls of the school. For example:
  * In the Voices and Memory module students gathered adolescents' perspectives on the September 11 disaster, which happened not far from the school. They compared these with other events in history; they used video conferencing to gather reactions from students in the United States and around the world and transcribed the interviews. The students presented their findings to the 9/11 museum board, where they will be will be on display at the opening. This module was carefully designed to develop knowledge of history, literature, psy-

chology, reading, writing, and other subjects in the standard curriculum, as well as 21st-century skills of group problem solving and information analysis.

* In the Green Roof module, groups of students designed a green roof for the 100-year-old building that housed the iSchool. They consulted with engineers, architects, and the city's department of education. They researched online the role of a roof in shelter and in the urban environment. Students' presented their fully developed solutions to the people in charge of replacing the roof. This challenge focused on the knowledge from the sciences, mathematics, and the arts, while developing skills in data analysis, group work, and decision making.

- Online instruction to master the traditional subject matter covered on the state Regents examinations. The online work enabled students to move through the material more quickly, at their own pace, with more interactivity and more opportunities for individual support. The faculty was able to target carefully what they needed to know for the test. Online coursework has also allowed the iSchool to expand what their small school course offers: AP courses, advanced subjects, and so forth. The courses material is available to students all day, every day, from school or from home, and includes many sample assessment activities drawn from questions on previous years' exams. A teacher is always available at the school for support as necessary.
- Core experiences. Not everything a student needs to know is best is learned through the challenge modules or the online courses. So students are scheduled for core experiences, such as science laboratories and Shakespeare seminars, led by a teacher and designed to develop not only the subject matter but the nature of student conduct in a serious classroom—an essential skill for success in college.
- Field experiences. Each student at the iSchool participates in an internship outside of the school. This required component helps nurture a spirit of community service, allows students to develop expertise in a specialized field, and lets them practice the social and workplace skills so important to success.
- Advisory. To provide the adult guidance so necessary to adolescent development, and to develop the meta cognition necessary to self-understanding, each student at the iSchool works with a faculty advisor. In the advisory period, students develop indi-

vidual learning plans in which they understand what they know, what they need to know, and how to learn it. Advisory helps students take more responsibility for their learning.

The Role of Technology

At the iSchool, digital networked technologies enable everything that students do. The school believes in ubiquitous access to technology and the information it brings to bear on the learning experience. The faculty did not simply place devices in the classroom, but thought differently about what how and where students could learn, and designed a system to let that happen. So the school's lessons are all posted on their Moodle learning management system, everything from readings to video clips to notes from the SmartBoard in the classroom. The Moodle has become a repository of curriculum materials developed by teachers: lessons, activities, resources, notes—all online for students, all the time. The online environment encourages teachers to build upon each other's work. A virtual desktop gives students access to their school files from anywhere. Each classroom houses 30 devices that can connect to the rest of the school (and to the world) through the wireless network that reaches into every classroom.

Results

Good news travels fast. The success of the iSchool in proving that a new model for high school can work has generated 1,500 applicants for the 100 seats in next year's entering class. Current students have worked through the required Regents material at a faster pace and with a higher pass rate. The iSchool's 95% attendance rate outshines the other high schools in the city. Scores on the parent and student satisfaction surveys conducted citywide show excellent results for this new and experimental approach. Parents report that students actually talk about their schoolwork at the dinner table. The connection between schoolwork and the real world figures strongly in the minds of these students.

Conditions for Success

A new learning approach is just part of the picture of success at the iSchool. Some of the contributing factors include:

- Coleadership. The principalship is shared by two leaders, who can apply four hands to the critical keys that need to be turned to make such a school work.

- Partnership with Cisco Systems. This corporate partner support-ed the school's vision, and helped the school find and configure the resources it needed to get started and to thrive.
- Department of Education support. The iSchool is part of the iZone, a conscious effort on the part of the New York City De-partment of Education to initiate and support high schools that work on innovative principles.
- On-site technical support. To keep all the computers and net-works working, and to help the teachers make the best use of them, knowledgeable people at the school site are essential.

The 25/C/1/1/1/6 plan for high school is not set in stone. For many students, it's not the best way to learn. And for the changing nature of the college and the workplace, it's probably not the best path of preparation. The success of the iSchool proves that other models can work. You can learn more about the iSchool at http://www.nycischool.org/

THE WATERSHED:
A CASE STUDY OF THE EDUCATION 3.0 PYRAMID IN PLAY

Killingly Intermediate School is located in a rural corner of northeast Con-necticut where the Quinebaug and Willimantic-Shetucket watersheds join to form the Thames River, which, in turn, leads to Long Island Sound. Water-powered factories and mills once formed the basis of the economy in the area. Some of the factories still exist. Though no longer water-pow-ered, they continue to influence the quality of the watershed and, eventu-ally, the Sound. Additionally, Native American tribes lived in and traveled through the area for many years. The history, science and stories of the area provide a rich opportunity for teachers to plan and deliver multidis-ciplinary, multiage, and multimedia curricula to their students. *Preserving Connecticut's Resources—Training Tomorrow's Stewards* is just such a project.

The project involves more than 150 students each year, challenging them to understand different aspects of the health of their watershed and its impact on the environment downstream. Each grade takes on one as-pect of the study, then comes together to present what they've learned and make recommendations to University of Connecticut (UConn) fac-ulty and the State Department of Environmental Protection. Annually, students produce videos, presentations, dances, music, and hardbound books, which serve as references for the next round of students.

In one recent year sixth graders told the story of a drop of water coming out of the faucet at home: where did it come from, where does it go? One student, Tré, had a plumber-grandfather who walked with him through the whole process, with Tré recording his grandpa's voice and shooting digital photos of each step, from the faucet, through the town sewer lines, to the water treatment plant, then onto the watershed. Later, Tré, who had always been labeled "learning disabled," produced a book in his own words to tell the story. He'll proudly show you the book, now in circulation in the school's library, ready for next year's language-challenged readers.

Killingly's seventh graders usually study Native American history of the area, in line with Connecticut's standard curriculum. For this project they focused on creation myths, then wrote their own myths involving water. Their part of the project included visits to local museums, interviews with the docents, creating original images to illustrate their hard-covered books for the school library. When it was time to present at the University of Connecticut, students could choose how they wanted to share what they'd done. One group choreographed a dance to tell its story. A musician in that group persuaded the school's jazz band teacher to help him write a musical score, then recorded the jazz band performing it. Another student, who has a passion for fabric arts, designed and made a costume based on historical references. Another group sought out the visual arts teacher to learn how to use PhotoShop to edit their images so they could show the gods weeping and creating rainbows on the earth.

One eighth-grade teacher, a former environmental water quality scientist, helped her students learn about, then use professional tools such as probes, microscopes, video cameras, and handheld GPSs to collect data on geography, weather, flora and fauna, geographical position, humidity, turbidity, density, pH, nitrates, coliform, and so on during several field trips along the watershed and out on Long Island Sound. This data was sent along to a national database for year-to-year comparisons and formed the basis of a video report presented at a UConn conference in the Spring. An eighth-grade English teacher linked the water study project to a poetry unit, challenging her students to see and describe water using a range of poetic forms. The result was a three-volume set of books now in circulation at both the intermediate and high schools that these students now attend. The freshmen English teachers use the poetry books in their courses.

This unit provides a good example of Education 3.0—or at least 2.75. The teachers worked as a team with their students to follow the general method of Education 3.0 (see Chapter 6):

- Confront a worthwhile problem (the quality of water in their neighborhood) through a range of lenses (science, history, writing, music, art)
- Seek out relevant ideas, facts, and skills that might help solve it

(probeware, data collection and analysis, technical skills such as PhotoShop, music composition)

- Gather, learn, and practice these ideas and skills (these became the basis of the curriculum throughout the spring);
- Apply them to the problem (using all the tools and skills in the field to gather the data)
- Publish a solution (presenting at conferences of professionals, publishing books, posting videos on the school web pages)

As the teachers reflect on the project, they realize some changes:

- Their role has changed: They work closely together to plan and coordinate lessons and activities, often via e-mail and after-school meetings; they work hard at developing collaborative environments for their students and themselves, encouraging students to seek out other adults in and out of school for support and information; They are no longer the sage on the stage.
- Students eagerly take more responsibility for their own learning, seeking others to help them as needed (the plumber-grandpa, the art teacher, the jazz band leader).
- They have a fuller range of assessments to understand what students have learned (one teacher does a pre- and post-KWL chart and has been astounded at the growth; others point to student projects, tests, and so forth to show growth; all have many points of measurement).

The pyramid has begun to reverse itself at Killingly Intermediate School. At least for this project, the teachers are drawing their curriculum from a carefully chosen and important problem, engaging all students in a variety of ways to solve and publish solutions for real audiences. And in doing so they learn all the basics along the way.

MESA

This large and diverse school district in Arizona formed a large and representative planning team to envision the future of their schools. Its 35 members included students, parents, board members, teachers, principals, technology staff, and the superintendent. Working in small groups, they created a vision for the future of their district, very much in line with Education 3.0. It provides a glimpse of school through the eyes of several different members of the educational community.

A Day in the Life at Mesa Schools

At Mesa Public Schools the needs of the student come first. As we transform our schools to meet those needs, we want to make sure that every student is prepared to learn, work, and contribute in this new century of ours. This means equal access to the information, ideas, and technologies that make the world tick. It means learning anywhere, anytime, in any setting. It means fostering innovation and initiative in all students.

What will these transformed schools look like?

Let's look through the eyes of five Mesa students, two teachers, a parent, a principal, and four musical instruments, and see what happens in a Day in the Life at Mesa schools.

Student 1: I am an eighth grader at Mesa Middle School. My day starts at home with an overview of my school task list—assignments, due dates, and things to be accomplished today. I get this list through an online system designed by the teachers that provides the information I need to be a successful student. It keeps me focused on what my teachers expect of me and helps with my time management. I make my own decisions about when to work on my independent projects. I often choose my own areas of interest to research. The handheld tablet on which I view my tasks also links to my assignments and to safe online resources.

I find my tasks online through the Mesa Schools Portal. My parents also can access this information from any device. In the portal I can access not only today's assignments, but my current grades, e-mail, homework, and school activities. A live streaming feed of information provides everything from current events discussions to school activities.

The portal is customized to my unique interests. I follow the volleyball team and the orchestra—those groups keep me updated on all their activities through the portal. There's a handy help button to assist me in anything I need. And the tracking feature is helpful. The trends in my achievement have been tracked since kindergarten, so I can see how I have done as I grow and learn through the curriculum.

My day at school begins at 8 a.m. The beginning of my day is open, allowing me to research and prepare for my current assignments. I really like having this part of my day flexible because that is when I am most alert and productive. (It's interesting—my friend likes her open time at the end of the day.) This morning, I am going to complete my Chinese link assignment. My day will include a blend of individual, small-group, and large-group collaboration. I love the individualized approach to my education. My tasks don't necessarily look exactly like my peers'. This is the way I love to learn!

Student 2: I am in first grade at Mesa Elementary School. We each carry an iPad that holds all our schoolwork and teaches us how to read. Yesterday I downloaded a book that I chose for myself. When I get home, Mom and Dad will read it to me from the iPad at bedtime.

I am really excited because next week it is my turn to make a podcast of the story that I wrote about bears. My teacher is going to help me. Everyone will see how well I write.

In school my teacher connects her iPad to the Smartboard so we can move the numbers around; this is called math, and I am beginning to understand it.

My family and I all get to use the iPad for a lot of different things. Last year I learned my ABC's and 123's on the iPad. This year my dad is practicing his English. My Mom likes to check my grades and check her recipes. My little sister is learning how to draw her letters and to take care of her puppy.

In school we learn how to use many different programs on our computers and iPads. If my phonics lesson is too hard, I can click on a link that shows my Mom and Dad how to help me at home. We learn world languages even in first grade. We use interactive words and pictures on our digital devices—here's the Chinese word for horse. Want to hear it? We can even connect to real Chinese people and talk with them. I love school so much. I might even want to grow up and be a teacher someday.

Student 3: I am an 11th-grade student. I begin my school day in the common room, where I connect to my personal online portal to check my schedule, chat with classmates, and review class notes. Students around me are doing many things: collaborating on a research project, video-chatting with their math tutor, and accessing textbooks on their portable devices.

Now I enter my Earth and Space Science class. Today we are studying the earth's divisions and their functions. In the front of the classroom a student leads a discussion, using Google Earth to describe the various components of the planet. Several study groups take part in the discussion while working at interactive computer tabletops, each interacting with a different part of the lesson. My group focuses on the location of populations. Group 2 looks at weather trends and their impact on people. Group 3 examines the polar ice cap and its effect on climate. Group 4 looks at natural disasters, weather, and climate. We all contribute to the discussion.

The whole lesson is being streamed live to other schools with whom we have been sharing resources. It's also being recorded for use by homebound or absent students. During all this, the teacher circulates, observes, monitors, facilitates discussion, and assesses what the students are learning.

On the football team this year we use interactive digital video to prepare for games. From the video equipment at the stadium—including cameras suspended on cables above the field—clips of the action are sent through the network to the school's online digital media library. From there the coach views it, and sends each of us the videos we need to review to improve our performance. We then try to match our on-screen performance with the animated playbook that also works on our various mobile devices—smartphone, tablet, computer. The same system provides real-time scores and live streaming video of all the games, so that my grandparents and others can watch from a distance.

Over the last 4 years I have been working on my College and Career Portfolio. It is a portrait of my accomplishments, skills, assignments, and activities during my high school career. My portfolio includes my SAT scores, projects, essays, scholarship info, ECAP (Arizona Education & Career Action Plan), FAFSA (Free Application for Federal Student Aid), video application, and resume. I will share all this online with the universities that I am interested in attending. The second portion of my portfolio tracks my college preparation progress. It alerts me to my testing and scholarship deadlines. It also includes an e-advisor that keeps track of my academic progress and how it will affect the college courses that I will take in the future. It communicates my progress to my parents and counselors and alerts them if I am struggling or not on schedule.

Teacher 1: I teach sixth grade at Mesa Elementary School. The use of technology has provided opportunities to make me more available to my students in a less formal setting. I am able to individualize their learning and provide more one-on-one instruction. I am also able to communicate on a daily basis with my students' parents as well as share their child's assessment results.

I often collaborate with teachers at my grade level where we use technology to review data and plan for large project-based assignments. I am able to assign online remediation lessons for struggling students. I use outside experts to teach my students in areas where my knowledge base is not as strong. We do this through interactive video conferencing and my students love guest lecturers. We also participate in virtual field trips all around the world.

Parent 1: I am a parent with a busy schedule. I need to know how and what my children are doing in a quick and efficient manner. I can access important information about their schoolwork through any Internet-connected device. Even though I work during school hours, that doesn't mean I can't be connected with the school. I stay in touch with teachers on a regular basis , though e-mail and video clips from my child's classroom. Even though I don't have Internet access at home, I often use the school's parent-access computers in the common room—these are available to us before, during, and after school.

Student 4: On the bus to school at 7 a.m., I listen to a podcast of my Spanish lesson. I need to learn the lesson on conjugating from present tense to past. We will have a quiz in class. Next to me, two friends work on a laptop collaborating on a biology presentation. They are combining data from last night's remote probe of the water quality in the canal closest to the school. Steven, our student community activist, is recording video of all of the drivers who pass the bus when the stop signs light are activated. It is part of a presentation he is developing for the Mesa City Council.

At the next stop we pick up two music students. They have an assignment to compose an original score for their music theory class. The score will be used in another group's video presentation. Randy hopes it is his presentation because he thinks the cellist is hot!

When I get to school, I'll have access to multiple resources to help me learn. When I am in class, I use laptops or handheld devices. My classes are constructed in such a way that I can work collaboratively and move my technology around, so I may work alone or with other students as necessary. For instance, in my group project for chemistry, I collaborate with four other students, each of us working on a different aspect of the project. We use iPads, smartphones, and laptops from home and school to connect with various online resources to do our chemistry assignment. Our teacher monitors us and checks our progress by viewing real-time screen shots of what we are doing and from what online resources we are getting our information.

My classroom includes a variety of seating options. In some places, I can stand at workstations. If I need to do productions or participate in a video activity, the school provides room for this kind of work. A teleconference screen in the room connects me with other people, if needed. I can even communicate with my teachers and people or places that are not in my classroom.

Additionally, we can connect to outside learning events in real time, which provide a more authentic learning experience. Today, my teacher is talking with an outside expert at another location. We see the expert herself on the big screen, she can see us, and she takes us on a tour of a museum that we are using for a deeper understanding of our history project. This environment allows us to study thematic units and integrate different learning disciplines.

Teacher 2: I am proud of the Westwood High School students in my Teacher Training class. They are working with the engineering students to develop lessons for third-grade students at our elementary feeder schools. Tomorrow they will travel to Emerson Elementary School and "teach" them minilessons. Group 1 will be learning vocabulary and terminology related to basic robotics and engineering concepts, using a Kindle. Group 2 will be tested on math proficiency using clickers on their iPads; and Group 3 will actually build the robots.

We share all this technology around the district from school to school, and the younger students enjoy the small-group instruction from the older students. High school students back at Westwood review the teaching of their peers, learning by watching their friends, and preparing for their own lesson that they will soon teach. Video conferencing provides the technology platform to ensure that everyone learns and benefits from various types of instruction.

Student 5: I broke my leg yesterday—skateboarding. I'm home in a cast, but I have complete access to everything going on at my high school. I log on to my laptop, where I see that most of my project group members—we are studying the impact of wild fires—are online. We talk about the information we gathered the night before, about costs, prevention, safety, environment, and possible careers. Even with my broken leg I can use the Mesa Schools Portal to keep up with my work, participate in interactive assignments, and ask questions in real time. I can even go to my counselor's page for information and advice. I can also work on my service learning project.

Here's today's spelling test on my tablet. I am competing as part of a group against three others to get the most points. All this happens online, and I can see my spelling tests since September, including a list of all the words I have missed this year. This helps me get better. As soon as the contest is over, I will congratulate the winning team through an instant message that will encourage them.

Over the past 2 weeks, I have been working on a group project that includes many different subjects. I know I have to master the state standards while doing these creative projects, and my student tablet allows me to see which standards I need to master for each of my core classes.

If the work I am doing on my projects is not helping me learn the standards, I can get all the help I need. My teacher can check on my progress via the Internet. I can click a link that gives me additional assignments for practice. I hope after I take my next online assessment, I will show mastery, but if I don't, I can get more help, perhaps a classmate who will work with me as a tutor—in person or online—to help me grasp the needed concepts.

If I still haven't mastered the standard, I will connect to a practice protocol that I am required to work on with my parents. My parents must document their time with me on my student portal. I may also be assigned to work with a group of students who have similar difficulties with the concept. My teacher will be in the room while I am working with my peers. What is great about this student tablet is I have control over what is happening to my learning. I know what I am missing, and I am guaranteed help in a variety of ways.

Principal 1: Our school includes a great deal of technology. We have access to phones, laptops, computers, iPads, iPods, and access to Facebook and Twitter. I want to make sure that there's a balance between the amount of communication that is happening between students, parents, and the school via technology and in person. I specifically want to create opportunities where people can talk directly with people. For example, we want to have opportunities for teachers to work with students in remediation. My parents want to be able to come to the school at night and meet with teachers in person, and we want to continue opportunities for students to participate in clubs, leadership, and drama, so they may learn important interpersonal skills.

Instrument 1: Trumpet. I am a trumpet in the junior high band. These are my stories. There is a trumpet player who has played the trumpet for 3 years and had private lessons. I like him. He is easy to work with, but next to him is a student who started only last year and needs lots of help. Fortunately, he can use a specialized program called Trumpet Hero, developed by a high school band student in New York for this specific music. My novice trumpeter can play along with the program and refine his techniques.

Instrument 2: Flute. Boy, do my flute players need instruction on breath control! It's not easy getting blown around all day by those kids. But things will get better—today they are watching the principal flutist from the National Symphony Orchestra of France demonstrating breath support and giving feedback—all done on the video conference screen.

Instrument 3: Piano. I have two student pianists who are challenging each other for first chair. As each one plays me, their work is recorded on a computer or iPad, then sent over the network to the school's digital media library, where the music teachers can listen to it and make their decision.

Instrument 4: Guitar. This student guitarist—the one with the sticky fingers—is uploading his final performance to his online portfolio. The recording will form the basis of his summative assessment and will be uploaded for his scholarship application for the Phoenix Youth Symphony.

All four instruments. The best part of our day is when we all come together—with all the students who play on us—for the last 30 minutes of each class to make music and band together.

TECH PARK HIGH SCHOOL

As they planned a new high school for this part of upstate New York, the superintendent, tech coordinator, librarians, and teachers followed an Education 3.0 approach. And they tell a good story, through the words of their hypothetical student, Sarah.

Workplace 1.0

Back then, we made our living from the land. In our part of New York, we plowed, planted, hayed, and harvested. We worked in small informal groups, using hand tools, and spent most of the day outdoors. All year long we grappled with nature, practiced our crafts, and learned from our elders the same skills they learned from theirs. Our workplace was the great outdoors, our dependencies rested on our neighbors and our kin, and life didn't change much from one generation to the next. We built our communities around the local resources, managing them to meet our local needs. The technologies of the day—the saw, the axe, the rake, the plow, the needle, and the Bible—were all we needed to make a living. We worked in small groups, old and young together. Let's call this Workplace 1.0, a static agricultural and artisanal culture firmly planted in the local landscape.

And our schools of that day reflected our workplaces: old and young studying together, using simple hand tools, preparing for the kind of work they'd find outside the schoolhouse door. We learned at school to use our hands, our legs, our bodies, and a bit of our minds to get done what needed to be done. We prepared our young people for the world they would inherit. Let's call this Education 1.0.

But change was in the air. As the 19th century ended and the 20th began, we saw new enterprises arise in our valleys and hillsides. We started to process our products in factories, so they could be sent to market by railroad. And so the nature of work changed. More of us worked inside the plant, fewer outside in the fields. We operated complex mechanical devices, with close tolerances and nonstop repetition. In Workplace 2.0, we became small cogs in a larger system of mass production, creating a uniform product that we would never use ourselves. We mastered the new technologies of the day to keep our businesses competitive. The small, informal work party evolved into an army of producers, some in factories, some in offices. We worked in large groups, closely supervised, following strict procedures, noses to the grindstone—or the pencil, or the typewriter, or the switchboard. We didn't talk much to each other—that would waste time. And time was of the essence in Workplace 2.0. The industrial revolution changed radically the way we worked, and called for a new set of skills and attitudes that the schools rapidly adapted to teach. In school we learned to sit up straight and not talk to our neighbors. We learned to work in large groups under close supervision, segregated by age, happy to all do the same thing at the same time—just as we would in the factories and offices into which we would graduate. We can call this Education 2.0.

Time was of the essence in the new school. So was uniformity, repetition, and obedience—the exact skills needed to succeed in Workplace 2.0. These Education 2.0 schools served us well right up through most of the 20th century. We added a few new technologies at the margins, but the basic structure and function of the school and the classroom did not change much.

But near the end of the century, the workplace began to change. Our mills and factories began to close down, as newer methods and foreign countries outproduced them. We built new kinds of businesses that extracted value from nature with radically new technologies. People worked not in large groups with mechanical tools, but in small groups with digital networked technologies. They combined information from many online sources, then sat down together to figure out how best to get the job done. Supervision was based on results—workers enjoyed the freedom to do what needs to be done to get the work accomplished. We invented new technologies that enabled us to do new kinds of work and demanded a new set of skills. We worked in small groups to identify and solve problems we had never seen before. We dealt with information from all over the world, arriving in our workplaces in real-time and forcing us to think quickly and in new and creative ways. Let's call this Workplace 3.0.

So the question before the house is, what kinds of schools do we need to prepare people to work in these kinds of settings? What should Education 3.0 look like? To answer this question, we'll follow Sarah through a day at Tech Park High School.

A Day in the Life at Tech Park High School

In the learning commons café to collaborate with her challenge group on their windmill project, Jill is looking for a morning snack. She uses her mobile device to text her order to the café ahead of time: almonds with berries. Immediately, she gets an analysis of the nutritional content, along with a suggestion that this snack will cost her 20 minutes on a treadmill. She texts the fitness center to schedule a treadmill for 20 minutes later that day. She also enters the calorie count into her online food profile.

> Health, wellness, and the whole child is supported by the school community.

As she pays for the snack in advance with the mobile device, a student from another work group asks her where the nuts and berries are from and whether they are safe and organic. Together they do some online research to compare her snack with a traditional industrial food snack. The other challenge group has been researching at a local farm the safety of food.

> Students solve authentic challenges, the same ones that people in business and industry and government are trying to solve. These problems involve the students in community service work in the community.

The two groups begin a discussion of food safety, schools snacks, and the effects of windmills on nearby livestock. Opinions fly fantastically, so they decide to seek expert advice from the extension specialist at Cornell. She appears on WebEx, and explains the role of pesticides on crop yields (positive) and windmills on livestock (unknown). The expert suggests a hydroponic experiment in pesticides for the students to carry out at school and points students to the relevant research on windmill effects. Meanwhile, others in the learning commons are reading and doing their work.

> Students engage in the upper levels of Bloom's taxonomy, constructing and presenting synthesis and conclusions. They employ the same video conferencing technologies used in business and industry.

As Jill leaves the learning commons, she sees on the digital signage board a display of what's happening today in school: student project work assignment postings; energy data from nearby turbines, solar cells, and geothermal probes. She is reminded to check quickly online from her iPad the output from the rooftop turbine that's generating power for the school greenhouse.

> Students and the school employ the same digital networked information tools that are used in universities and businesses.

Students collaborate with each other using a variety of fixed and mobile technologies to find solutions to those problems.

Jill passes eight students meeting with their faculty coach in a small conference room off the learning commons. A local farm owner, concerned about rising fuel prices and difficult delivery schedules, has come to them to research whether her farm could go off the grid through wind energy. She strikes them as a rugged individualist. The group draws up a plan to put some online environmental measuring devices at the farm, from which they will remotely read data on wind, sun, and geothermal activity.

Students interact with industry experts and local businesses.

Their faculty coach, a social studies teacher, texts a colleague in math to schedule a direct instruction lesson on data sampling techniques and regression analysis for 2 weeks hence, when the farm data become available. Meanwhile two other members of the group research the state and local regulations on installing turbines, while three others meet with state environmental officials over WebEx from the small conference room.

Students use online research sources to gather information they need for their academic projects, just in time.

Next day in their English class, they are assigned to read the essay *Self-Reliance* by R. W. Emerson, and the poem "No Man is an Island" by John Donne. Evidently the English teacher has been conspiring with the faculty coach. After class, the challenge group meets again to divide up their tasks: One will construct a slide presentation on changing regulations for backyard turbines; two will meet with the loan officer in the adjacent bank branch to learn the possibilities for a farmer to borrow money for such a project; two more will approach the student-managers of the school café to see how the farm might serve as a supplier of lettuce and tomatoes.; and one will consult with the school's work-study coordinator to solicit students to work on the farm to try a new way to grow lettuce & tomatoes.

Students solve authentic challenges, the same ones that people in business and industry and government are trying to solve. These problems involve the students in community service work in the community.

The student manager of the café rolls the portable cooking lab out to the patio adjacent to the learning commons to conduct a demonstration on grilling local vegetables,which he will sell when they are done. At the same time in the commons' small performance area, a challenge group is finishing up its presentation of the final report of its research project. As they clear out, a student jazz quartet moves its instruments into place.

After the jazz, one of the teachers will use the same spot to present a lecture on recent advances in photovoltaic technology. Across the commons, Jill sees a student reading in a chair with good light and pleasant plants. Another works on a laptop at a chair with a tray specially designed for this purpose. She watches another student borrow a camera to take photographs of the farm's potential turbine site.

> Students work in spaces designed specifically for 21st-century schoolwork.

The digital signage board has changed: It's showing an announcement for tonight's concert of student-composed original music, followed by a student video production about the upcoming local election. Looking left through the soundproof glass she sees the video producers in the digital studio putting the final touches on their project, which they will soon send up to the Show-and-Share digital media library.

In Jill's Advanced Placement English literature class, students apply a critical lens to Rachel Carson's *Silent Spring*. Today's class is led by the librarian; this freed up the English teacher to take another group on a field trip to a local pond very much like Walden Pond in Massachusetts. You can imagine which book they're reading!

> Disciplines are integrated and balanced to get core academic requirements as well as higher level skills.

After the class takes some self-correcting online Regents exam practice questions on critical lenses, the librarian sends Jill and two colleagues off online to find historical news reports from the 1960s contemporary with Carson's work. From these, Jill will prepare a presentation that relates the book to current-day issues.

> State learning standards and college preparation are integrated throughout the students' days.

In her Living Environments class, Jill learns how to design and experiment in hydroponic vegetable growing. She plans an experiment that will help her food safety project. At the end of class, the teacher reviews on the SmartBoard sample Regents test questions on experimental design. As the teacher posts the multiple-choice questions, the students' responses (tapped on their iPods) are reflected as a graph on the SmartBoard.

At lunch in the learning commons, Jill sees a science teacher, an English teacher, and the librarian collaborating to design new competencies for the students' portfolios. As they work, students drop by and ask for help in their project. A parent of one of Jill's friends walks in with the farmer we met earlier to buy lunch at the café, where they meet with the students who will be working on the farm project.

Teachers are conspiratorial architects, working collaboratively to plan learning experiences for their students. A nurturing environment fosters healthy faculty-student relationships.

How-to Guidance for Slide Shows and Podcasts

SLIDE SHOW PRODUCTION

In Chapter 2 you need to turn your sketches and scripts of your *Day in the Life* into a slide show suitable for presentation to the various constituencies in the school community. The most effective presentations consist of images with little or no text, a very different type of slide show from the kind that most people are used to. Follow these step-by-step instructions to build the slide show.

1. Launch your presentation program. On Macintosh, use Keynote; on Windows, PowerPoint. You will find Keynote easier to use with video and images and saving as a podcast.
2. Choose a plain background. This will help your audience focus on your message without the distraction of cute backdrops and fancy fonts. Plain white, black, or gray works best.
3. On the first slide, add a text box and enter the title: *A Day in the Life at (school name) School.*
4. Add or insert a blank slide.
5. Add a text box to this slide, and into it enter the time of the first event in the day, such as "6:30 a.m."
6. Move the text box to one of the corners of the slide.
7. Add an image to the slide.
   a. In PowerPoint, choose Insert —> Photo —> Picture from file.
   b. In Keynote, open the Media Browser and drag the item into the slide.
   c. Let the image fill the screen, bleeding off to the edges.
8. Duplicate this slide.
9. Remove the image or video.
10. Change the time for the next event in the text box.

11. Repeat Step 7.
12. Continue with steps 8–11 until you have used all your images.

You may be tempted by habit to put additional text onto the slides. Don't do it. When the slides are presented in a podcast, your voice will carry the verbal message. When you publish the vision in a variety of formats, one of those will include the written text.

PODCAST PRODUCTION

To develop your slides into a podcast, you'll need to plan the narration, rehearse the narration, and record the narration. Follow these general instructions to build the podcast.

1. Think silently.
   a. Display the slides to the entire group, holding each one in place for ten seconds.
   b. As each slide is displayed, ask participants to compose in their minds the narration for this slide.
2. Discuss orally.
   a. Again display the slides in turn, letting the group discuss the best type of narration for each slide.
   b. Don't write it down—keep this discussion oral.
   c. As soon as the group agrees on the narration for each slide, go to the next.
3. Appoint a narrator.
   a. Let the group chose the person with the most natural voice to narrate the show.
   b. The best narrators can work ex tempore, from memory, without written notes.
4. Rehearse the narration.
   a. Let the narrator in front of the group speak to each slide as it is displayed, then let the group suggest improvements.
   b. After the first pass, let the narrator make a second continuous pass, narrating this time without comment.
   c. Listen to Franklin Roosevelt's fireside chats for a good example of a speaking style appropriate to a podcast.
   d. Speak up when you record, close to the microphone, but don't pretend you are lecturing. Instead, pretend the listener is sitting across the table from you when you speak.

5. Record the narration.
   a. Send the narrator off to a quiet room to record the narration.
   b. Use Keynote or PowerPoint software to record your narration (specific instructions are found below).

Here are step-by-step instructions for recording the narration in Keynote:

1. Choose File —> Record Slideshow from the menubar.
2. The slide show will play; as it does, speak your narration into the built-in microphone.
3. Click through the slides as you record.
4. Export your work as a podcast.
5. If you need to edit your finished podcast, you may use iMovie. But it may be faster just to go back and re-record the narration in Keynote, and save again when you are done.

Here are step-by-step instructions for recording the narration in PowerPoint:

1. Choose Slideshow —> Record Slideshow from the menubar.
2. The slide show will play; as it does, speak your narration into the built-in microphone.
3. Click through the slides as you record.
4. Save your work as a movie.

Articles on the Mobile Device Controversy

- Are you ready for mobile learning? http://www.educause.edu/EDUCAUSE+Quarterly/EDUCAUSEQuarterlyMagazineVolum/AreYouReadyforMobileLearning/157455
- Pros and cons of iPods in school. http://ezinearticles.com/?Pros-and-Cons-of-iPods-in-School&id=1922814
- The mobile curriculum. http://www.powertolearn.com/articles/teaching_with_technology/article.shtml?ID=105
- New iPod rules touch off heated debate. http://www.eschoolnews.com/news/top-news/?i=58886
- No iPod, Blackberry use in school proposed. http://www.wickedlocal.com/weymouth/news/x702317041/No-ipod-blackberry-use-in-school-proposed
- An iPod for school? http://atlantis2.cbsnews.com/video/watch/?id=3244378n
- High-tech cheating: What every parent needs to know. http://www.commonsensemedia.org/hi-tech-cheating
- Mobile devices: Facing challenges and opportunities for learning. http://thejournal.com/articles/2009/03/19/mobile-devices-facing-challenges-and-opportunities-for-learning.aspx
- Northridge electronic devices policy. http://www.davis.k12.ut.us/schools/nhs/files/DD0AD8E18BE746F-997B0217A2012A3B4.pdf
- iPod touch: Touching student lives in the classroom. http://edcommunity.apple.com/ali/story.php?itemID=16472
- Library in a pocket. http://www.nytimes.com/2009/11/18/technology/18reader.html?_r=1&scp=1&sq=novels&st=cse

Notes

Introduction

1. C. B. Swanson, *Cities in Crisis 2009: Closing the Graduation Gap,* (Bethesda, MD: Editorial Projects in Education, 2009).

2. E. Yazzie-Mintz, *Charting the Path from Engagement to Achievement: A Report on the 2009 High School Survey of Student Engagement,* (Bloomington, IN: Indiana University, Center for Evaluation & Education Policy, 2010).

3. S. Dorn, "High-Stakes Testing and the History of Graduation," *Education Policy Analysis Archives, 11*(1), January 2003.

4. See, for instance, "Schools Chief's Truck Vandalized Amid Reform Furor," February 15, 2011, *Standard Journal.* Retrieved from http://www.rexburgstandardjournal.com/news/schools-chief-s-truck-vandalized-amid-reform-furor/article_0968677a-3946-11e0-8095-001cc4c03286.html?mode=story#axzz1ylaBvBR8

5. *Charting the Path from Engagement to Achievement: A Report on the 2009 High School Survey of Student Engagement,* (Bloomington, IN: Center for Evaluation & Education Policy, Indiana University, 2010).

6. Tony Wagner, *The Global Achievement Gap* (New York: Basic Books, 2010).

Chapter 1

1. D. H. Autor, F. Levy, & R. J. Murnane, "The Skill Content of Recent Technological Change: An Empirical Exploration," *Quarterly Journal of Economics, 118*(4), 2003, p. 1284.

2. Ibid.

3. Cisco Systems, *The Learning Society* (San Jose, CA: Author, 2009), p. 7.

4. According to the U.S. Census Bureau's American Community Survey, the median income for a family of four in 2010 was $60,000. Earning $30 per hour over 40 hours per week for 50 weeks provides that level of income.

5. J. H. Dyer, H. B. Gregersen, & C. M. Christensen, *The Innovator's DNA: Mastering the Five Skills of Disruptive Innovators* (Boston, MA: Harvard Business School Press, 2011), pp. 23, 24, and 89.

6. National Research Council, *Education for Life and Work: Developing Transferable Knowledge and Skills in the 21st Century.* Committee on Defining Deeper Learning and 21st Century Skills, James W. Pellegrino and Margaret L. Hilton, Editors. Board on Testing and Assessment and Board on Science Education, Division of

Behavioral and Social Sciences and Education. (Washington, DC: The National Academies Press, 2012).

7. *Walden: A Fully Annotated Edition* (New Haven, CT: Yale University Press, 2004), p. 54.

8. Thoreau's letter to Orestes Brownson, 30 December 1837, quoted in *Uncommon Learning: Thoreau on Education,* Martin Bickman, ed. (New York: Houghton Mifflin Harcourt, 1999), p. xviii.

9. *The McGuffey Readers*, 1836 version, McGuffey Readers World (n.d.). Retrieved from http://www.mcguffeyreaders.com/1836_original.htm

10. Henry Petrovsky, *The Pencil: A History of Design and Circumstance* (New York: Knopf, 1992).

Chapter 6

1. Galileo Galilei, *The Assayer,* trans. Stillman Drake, in *Discoveries and Opinions of Galileo* (New York: Anchor, 1957), pp. 237–238.

2. Grant Wiggins, "The Common-Core Math Standards: They Don't Add Up," September 28, 2011, *Education Week, 31*(5), p. 22.

Credits

Grateful acknowledgment is made for permission to reprint the following:

Figures I.1, 1.16, 1.17, 2.1, and 2.2: Photos and drawings courtesy of the author.

Table 1.1: From D. Gilbert (2008), *The American Class Structure in an Age of Growing Inequality*. Sage Publications, Inc., London. Used with permission.

Figure 1.1: *Waiting for an Answer,* Winslow Homer. Used with permission of the Maryland State Archives.

Figure 1.2: *Breezing Up (A Fair Wind),* Winslow Homer. Courtesy of the National Gallery of Art, Washington.

Figure 1.3: *Snap the Whip,* Winslow Homer. Used with permission of the Butler Institute of American Art, Youngstown, OH.

Figure 1.4: *The Country School,* Winslow Homer. Used with permission of the Saint Louis Art Museum, St. Louis, MO.

Figure 1.5: Photo courtesy of the Florida History Internet Center.

Figure 1.6: Photo courtesy of the Carlow County Museum, Carlow Town, Ireland (www.carlowcountymuseum.ie).

Figure 1.7: Photo courtesy of the Early Office Museum (www.officemuseum.org).

Figure 1.8: Photo used with permission of www.duryeapa.com.

Figure 1.9: Photo used with permission of the Richland County Genealogical Society, Ohio.

Figures 1.10–1.11 and 1.13–1.15: Photos licensed and used with permission of iStockphoto.

Figure 1.12: Used with permission of the Independent Electricity System Operator (IESO), Ontario.

Figure 1.18: From D. Autor (2001), "The Skill Content of Recent Technological Change," National Bureau of Economic Research, working paper 8337. Used with permission of the author.

Figure 4.2: From OECD (2009), "Take the Test: Sample Questions from OECD's PISA Assessments," PISA, OCED Publishing: http://dx.doi.org/10.1787/9789264050815-en. Used with permission.

Index

About the Author

Jim Lengel earned his degrees at Yale College and the Harvard Graduate School of Education, and has worked in government, academic, and industry organizations for 42 years. After serving as a Peace Corps volunteer teacher in the Marshall Islands, Jim began his career as a public school teacher in Vermont, where he worked his way to the post of Deputy Commissioner of Education, and was appointed to a Fulbright Scholarship in China. His interest in new technologies led him to Apple Computer, where he served as Education Technology Consultant for 6 years. Jim returned to teaching at Boston University, where he developed the digital media program at the College of Communication, and helped build a center for teaching excellence. He is currently on the faculty of Hunter College of the City University of New York, where his work concentrates on the application of digital technologies to teaching and learning. Jim consults with organizations around the world on this topic, including the University of Nantes in France, the South China University of Technology, Apple Computer, Cisco Systems, Cablevision, and dozens of schools and colleges. Jim has authored eight books on education and communication, including Addison-Wesley's *Guide to Web Design,* and Allyn & Bacon's *Integrating Technology: A Practical Guide.* Jim publishes a weekly column and podcast on teaching with technology at PowerToLearn.com. He is licensed by the U.S. Coast Guard as a Captain in the Merchant Marine, and races his yawl *Top Cat* along the coast of New England during the summer season. He can be reached at jim@lengel.net.